MEN AND BRETHREN

Books by James Gould Cozzens

S.S. SAN PEDRO
1931

THE LAST ADAM
1933

CASTAWAY
1934

MEN AND BRETHREN
1936

ASK ME TOMORROW: *or* YOUNG FORTUNATUS
1940

THE JUST AND THE UNJUST
1942

GUARD OF HONOR
1948

BY LOVE POSSESSED
1957

CHILDREN AND OTHERS
1964

MORNING NOON AND NIGHT
1968

Therefore let all the house of Israel know assuredly, that God hath made that same Jesus, whom ye have crucified, both Lord and Christ.

Now when they heard this, they were pricked in their heart, and said unto Peter and to the rest of the apostles, Men and brethren, what shall we do?

THE ACTS OF THE APOSTLES, 2:36, 37

JAMES GOULD COZZENS

Men and Brethren

HARCOURT BRACE JOVANOVICH, INC., NEW YORK

MEN AND BRETHREN

ONE

T HE TELEPHONE was ringing. Ernest let the ringing go on while he searched for a cigarette. Taking one from the package he found, he put it in the corner of his mouth and began a second search, for matches. Before he found them, he heard Lily take the call in the basement. Her piercing, aged, negroid voice chanted: "Saint Ambrose's Vicarage."

Ernest lit the cigarette, filled his lungs with smoke, and dropped on the edge of the low divan bed. "Mr. Cudlipp!" Lily's voice climbed shrilly. "Mr. Cudlipp!"

"All right!" he shouted. He plucked the instrument off the stand, lay back against the cushions, at the same time picking up the scraps of paper with penciled messages which had been left on the table.

"Ernest Cudlipp speaking," he said. The cigarette in the corner of his lips nodded lightly to the words. From Lily's execrable writing he learned that Doctor Lamb had called. Doctor Lamb would stop by about half past ten.

Ernest sighed. He could have guessed that from the glimpse of Mr. Hurst's car drawing up in refined splendor

3

at the arches of the Parish House door just as Ernest left. The Senior Warden, at some sacrifice of his personal convenience, almost always got in Fridays—even as hot a Friday as this. Told all, Mr. Hurst had protested. Mr. Hurst would point out that the Bishop wouldn't like it. What would be the use? Holy Innocents' was not the sort of parish which relished a good rousing row. Mr. Cudlipp wasn't down at Saint Matthew's now. Let him attend to the work for which Holy Innocents' in its pious generosity had built and maintained the Chapel, and stop trying to—

From the telephone a voice said: "Oh, Ernie! I've got to see you. I've really got to."

Ernest tossed the first note aside and held up the second. "I'm sorry," he said, perplexed by Lily's spelling—Lord, it must be Lulu Merrick! She must have managed to get to town again. He inhaled smoke wearily. "I'm sorry," he repeated, "this is a very bad connection. I don't know who you are."

"Oh. It's Geraldine. Mrs. Binney."

"Of course. Now, what are you crying about, and why do you have to see me?"

"I can't tell you on the phone. May I come down?"

The third slip was in John's writing: *Took five dollars out of your top drawer—J.*

"No, Geraldine," he said. "I've a dinner engagement. If you want to see me, I'll come up there about half past nine." The cigarette, consuming itself, shortened. He narrowed his right eye against the smoke streaming thinly past it, squinted with his left, reading on the last slip: *Dear Vicar. Mrs. Hawley very low in mind, though doctor says not immediate danger. Would like to see you personally if possible—Johnston.*

"Yes," he said into the phone. "I want to have a talk with you, too, Geraldine. I've been meaning to have one for some time."

4

"Oh. What about?"

"About what you've got to see me about, I think. Now, go lie down."

"Ernie, what's happened to him?"

"Nothing. He's perfectly all right. I haven't seen him today, but there was a note from him."

"What did he say—oh. I'm sorry."

"Don't be. He said he was borrowing five dollars. He's perfectly all right. And so are you, Geraldine. Nine-thirty, or near it. God bless you." He dropped the telephone on the stand, stood up, picking away the hot fragment of cigarette from his lips, and lit another.

Although it was after half past six, and the sun was in merciful decline, no breeze stirred. From the tall old-fashioned windows of his bedroom Ernest Cudlipp could see the narrow, barren backyards divided monotonously by broken, disproportionately high, board fences. Through them, a rank diseased growth of ailanthus trees distributed itself, sickly fronds lifted high into the maze of clotheslines strung from flat windows to lofty bare poles. Every pole was more or less off the perpendicular. A shadow smelling of hot stone, hot rubbish, burnt gasoline, filled the disreputable interior of the block. Invisible, an elevated train passed. Its low roar came leisurely in hollow crescendo. Then it went deliberately, dying away downtown.

Ernest thumbed loose his clerical collar and detached the black linen stock, sailing them onto the top of the bureau stacked with books. At the window again, Ernest saw young Munson, his organist, come out the back two stories under him, proceed down the yard and through the gate. Munson had his shirt sleeves rolled up on his long pallid forearms and carried several bound scores. From his work as a sales clerk in a haberdashery store he came directly, hot and winded, to his real love. The gate banged. Mun-

5

son passed with brisk little footfalls along the grimy flank of Saint Ambrose's Chapel, trotted down the cement entryway, and into the choir room.

Ernest took off his trousers, pulled his damp shirt over his head, dropping both on a chair. He was waiting, curious to hear what Munson began with. Munson had a developed taste in music, an admirable touch, and a minor, pleasant talent as a composer. It was perhaps a pity that he couldn't be paid enough to make selling neckties unnecessary; but, as likely as not, if he had more time, he would use it with less desperate devotion, do actually less work.

Ventilating sections of the ugly stained glass were tilted open behind the metal netting which covered the Chapel windows, and the low hum of electric power at the pump arose audibly. In the organ loft Munson touched his banked keys. Irrelevant, deep, sustained and sad, a B-minor chord sounded; steady, mechanically prolonged. There was silence. Then with a resolute whoop, sobering to patient purpose, the first sententious notes of Bishop Doane's hymn for the Missions surged over the backyards.

Ernest shook his head, recognizing Munson's rigid selection of duty before pleasure. On an evening as hot as this, duties of that lamentable sort must be almost beyond a musician's endurance. Mr. Johnston was to preach Sunday and the hymn was a favorite of his. Ernest shook his head again. He went in and turned on a shower.

"Fling out the banner," he found himself unwillingly echoing, "let it float, Seaward and skyward, high and wide —" But no, no! What senseless bombast! Angels did well to bend in anxious silence o'er the sign! There were no banners about poor Mr. Johnston. The nations, crowding to be born—did Eskimos crowd to Mr. Johnston to be born? More likely, Mr. Johnston crowded to them. From them he took reality, all that could be called his life.

In the narrow loop of a parka hood unimaginable cold

6

had calloused Mr. Johnston's forehead and cheeks. Of course he had worn a beard, Ernest realized suddenly. Mr. Johnston must have shaved it off because, no doubt largely white, it would make him look older than the hills. Mr. Johnston's eyes had been irreparably injured by snow glare. Ringed with the horn rims of his thick glasses, the lids were red, the magnified blue irises bleached. When he spoke his voice croaked weak and stiff. He often hesitated and stammered, as though his tongue, more familiar with —was it fourteen?—Indian and Eskimo dialects, became uncertain and diffident, trying English. The sermon Sunday would necessarily be a horror, a genuine horror. He oughtn't to attempt it. Only, you could see, Mr. Johnston thought that if he didn't try, he'd never be able to resume preaching. He went at it with all his might; just as, eagerly, he made his round of calls with an awkward resolution easy to picture—the confused greetings, the stiff halting conversations, the embarrassed, probably too long delayed leave-takings. Mr. Johnston was determined to master the routine work of a city priest, to be useful to the Vicar, to justify his position.

Of course Mr. Johnston never could. He was hopeless. Even with a person of young Wilber Quinn's vast energy over from General Seminary—he was an ordained graduate student, full of the enthusiasm of his inexperience—to help out, the regular summer work didn't get done. In the fall, the work would never get done. The position of an Episcopal chapel in a district like this depended almost too plainly on the things, paid for out of the ample purse of Holy Innocents', which Saint Ambrose's could offer— the day nurseries and the dispensaries, the Chapel House activities, the summer camps. If more were to be accomplished, the clergy in charge had to accomplish it entirely through their own personalities.

Mr. Johnston's personality was negative, for this purpose practically non-existent. For twenty-five years he had brought the Gospel to southern Alaska and the Yukon Territory—to God, the doubtful glory; to him, largely destroyed eyesight; a ruined constitution; worst of all, what really seemed to be a mental impairment, a simplicity very close to silliness. No longer young or strong enough to continue working where his experience had value, where he could do what few white priests could, Mr. Johnston came back, tremulous and rheumy, almost provisionless, with few friends, with no abilities— Ernest stepped from the shower, turned a towel about his short compact body, and shining with cool water, went into his bedroom.

Lee Breen had said seven, naming the pretentious hotel where he was accustomed to stop because his reputation was good there for a great reduction in rates. It seemed hard to believe, but there really must be people who would go to a hotel in order to see Lee, or someone like him, in the lobby. Ernest tried to imagine who they were. He got into shorts and a shirt, lit a cigarette, and took up a new quarto of German photographs of baroque and rococo churches—at Quito, Ecuador, the Compañía's carved and crusted doorway. Inside, solid gold plated every wall —trust the Jesuits! But here was San Francisco of Quito, the Friars Minor enthroned in dispendious humility. Trust them all! He studied the low decorated tower caps, the rich eruption of stonework on the square façade, the divided stairs rising in dignity from left and right.

Flipping over the page, he paused, arrested, for Munson, duties done, suffused the evening air with Bach. The Saint John Passion flooded the backyards. With impressive skill, Munson was adapting for his organ the great contralto air, *Es ist vollbracht,* counterpointed with a simulated cello accompaniment.

Ernest breathed deeper, satisfied. He began to sing,

8

though he knew almost none of the German wording, and could not even be sure which were the voice parts. Sharply up the shadowed stairway cut the telephone bell. "Ta-ti-tum, ta; ta-tum—" he intoned, pulling a shirt over his head. He jammed his hands down the sleeves, his head emerged, thin brown hair upended, through the neck. He swung out an arm and caught off the telephone. "Ernest Cudlipp speaking."

Lee Breen's clean, clear stage enunciation broke out, impatient. "Ernest, are you dead? Do you know what time it is?"

"To the minute," he answered. "Seven-thirty-two."

"Well, come at once! Meyer may ring me. If he does, I'll have to go. I told you that."

"As soon as I get my trousers on. Alice isn't ready, is she?"

"Of course she is. And being very nasty, too."

"Lord, apologize for me, will you? Tell her I'll see she has a dinner fit to eat finally."

"Now, Ernest, we're going to eat here. I haven't time to go out—"

"No, we're not. I shall probably die in a year or two and I'm not going to waste any of my few remaining meals swallowing gilded swill." He hung up, went into the hall and shouted, "Lily, get me a taxi!" Returning, he flung out on the bed a gray suit of thin flannel, bent, and spun the telephone dial. "Joseph," he said, "this is Mr. Cudlipp. Have a wonderful dinner for three for me a little after eight, and a cold wine. No, I don't want to hear about it now, I want to eat it when I get there. Yes." He tossed back the telephone.

As though in protest, it immediately rang again.

"Mr. Cudlipp, this is Bill Jennings. I tried to call but the line was busy."

9

"Yes." Ernest let his eyes rest on the very old, much battered, but how beautifully executed, wooden figure of Saint Ambrose standing on the little shelf built for it in the high corner of the room. On the left arm a miniature Milan cathedral was held to the heart. The feet were on the beehive, the scroll of the *Te Deum* was broken off in the right hand. It was oak, about four feet high—supposedly thirteenth-century work, and Lee, who had brought it back to him from Italy several years ago, must have paid a good deal for it.

"Well, what happened, sir, I found out, was that the crazy kid sent a money order to this firm—they advertise you can do that—for this revolver. It comes insured or registered, or something, so he has to sign for it. At the post office, they must tip them off; because, right away, as soon as Jimmy signs and the man gives it to him, a plain-clothes man pinches him for violation of the Sullivan law—"

"He's still a minor, isn't he?"

"Well, he's eighteen, Mr. Cudlipp. They can send him to Sing Sing, I think. They're holding him for bail."

Ernest removed his eyes from Saint Ambrose's hoary haloed head. "Don't try to raise it. It might scare some sense into him to stay in jail a few days. But try not to let your father worry. I think we can get him out of it."

"Taxi's waiting, Mr. Cudlipp," Lily screamed.

"If there's anything else, call me again, later. Or I'll see you at the office in the morning. I can't stay now." He hung up, snatched a black knitted tie, knotted it under the attached collar of his soft shirt. He swung on the flannel coat, and clapping a panama on his head, ran downstairs. "Lily!" he said, "I'll try to be back at ten or a little after. If Mr. Quinn calls up, or comes in, tell him he needn't bother about the early service Sunday. I'll take it myself. But he must be sure I have a server, because there probably won't be anyone else there. Do you hear me?"

"Yes, Mr. Cudlipp. I hear you."

Ernest ran on down the brownstone front steps. The taxi driver opened the door and he scrambled in. "I'm in a hurry," he said. "Don't be too careful, it makes me nervous."

Four blocks west, the sun, slanting level through the great cleft of buildings, shafted across the avenue to fall on the fine Byzantine masses of the new Holy Innocents'. Reclining in his corner, Ernest gazed out the open taxi window at it, pleased—the solemn strong nave, the strong low dome of plain pendentives and sweeping smooth cupola on the crossing—it couldn't be better.

Halted at the corner, he could observe the serenely balanced west front, the sunlight falling on the thick stone spokes of the big west window; the partly dismantled scaffolding around the porch. The porch and portals had just been added to complete the new building on the one hundredth anniversary of the founding of the parish. In the shadow of the remaining framework, three pairs of magnificent bronze doors were now in place. Above them, above the small triple pillars of colored marble, the entablature was uncovered. On it, cut in a narrow diaglyphic band, the collect for the feast ran graven in stone. The effect was going to be good; but what a collect! *O Almighty God*—the noble letters marched from the side and turned across the front—*who out of the mouths of babes and sucklings hast ordained strength, and madest infants to glorify thee by their deaths; Mortify and kill all vices in us. . . .*

Really, 'madest infants to glorify thee by their deaths'! For once Doctor Lamb had clearly and unquestionably been caught napping. Wait until the scaffolding was finally cleared away next week and the old ladies got a good look at it! Ernest was willing to bet that within six months the lettering would be quietly effaced as the only possible way of keeping the parish peace. Now going south on the avenue he got a last glimpse—the bulk of the Parish House behind the church, and on the street below, Mr. Hurst's big car still waiting at the entrance vaults—Ernest wouldn't flatter himself by supposing that all this time had been spent on objections to the conduct of affairs at Saint Ambrose's, but no doubt it was objection of some sort to parish affairs of some kind. "As rector of a parish like this, I wouldn't last a year," Ernest reflected; "the truth is, I have no tact. It isn't that I wouldn't stand for it, it's that I couldn't. I don't know how."

Once, the lack of the knowledge might have seemed to him a kind of compliment to some imaginary integrity; but now he could see it well enough as the flaw that it was, a defect in self-control—the scriptural dangers of judgment, of council, of hell-fire. He thought, "In forty-four—well, practically forty-five—years I have never found out how to agree with mine adversary quickly. That is really why I am where I am, why I will never be—"

But he was there, he saw. In the lobby he went briskly down to the bar and glanced in. It was crowded, but there was no sign of Lee or Alice. Back at the long, bright, ornate desk, they pushed a telephone over to him. Leaning on his elbows, he heard it answered finally. Alice said: "What?"

"Come down and eat."

"Hello, Ernie. I don't think I will. Where's Lee?"

"I haven't the faintest idea."

"Oh. Well, I suppose Meyer came around for him. All right, darling. I'll come."

"Did you have a row?"

"Nothing special. Only I don't like to be called a dirty little slut in public. It's partly your fault for being so late."

"Well, come on, my dear. It's getting later."

He crossed the lobby and sat down where he could see the elevator doors. He sat there, glum, because he was hungry—or was it because Lee depressed him, as a type or example? Lee must be thirty-eight or nine and you couldn't expect him to remain, in spite of it, a perpetual twenty-five. At twenty-five Lee had been intelligent, modest, unaffected; so time could not change him, as it changed many people of twenty-five, for the better. If Lee changed, he had to change for the worse. His success assured it. In the theater, the place where there was plenty of room was at the bottom, not at the top. Only at the bottom was there leisure to be simple and natural, elbow-room to be generous and good-tempered. "The good old days!" Ernest thought, and the thought was derisive; for no one knew better than himself what a delusion that was. Yet the discouraged sense of them persisted—all the old days done with, all the charming people gone, or different; the hopes exploded, the exciting plans found only fatuous or ill-considered. In the distance he saw a pair of gilded elevator doors spring open. Alice stepped out.

Ernest remembered with surprise that he had originally disliked Alice. As an actress she had been a thoroughly bad one. No one could help agreeing about that, except, apparently, Alice herself; but the first little theaters gladly accepted her. She had money, and could be counted on to contribute toward the productions.

If on the stage there was little to recommend Alice, off it there was even less. She had represented, in the silliest and most blatant possible way, a definite type then coming to town in force. Her father was a Methodist minister in some small city. Alice had fretted through a temperamental adolescence there; but soon she would probably have settled down, taught by ordinary experience that never had there been and never would there be any such world as the one she wanted to go out and live in. As Ernest remembered it, her going out had been an unfortunate accident, result of some complicated series of deaths and family quarrels, which made her the heir of an uncle, her mother's brother. She was free at eighteen or nineteen, and able to see herself as a gallant fugitive from her father's Methodism, from her town's indifference to all the finer things of life.

If he had ever known them, Ernest had forgotten the exact circumstances—whether it was Lee who interested her in the theater, whether interested in the theater, she met Lee; whether he met her through Lee, or whether, with so many other queer people, she had turned up at Doctor Ogilvie's circuses at Saint Matthew's. But he did remember that she could only be described as awful. Loud and resolute, Alice got drunk with the best of them. Frank and forthright, she employed frequently all the improper words she knew without turning a hair. Soon she was playing out the short, dreary, absurd gamut of what she hoped was sin. No doubt she tried cocaine. Certainly she began to claim that her sexual experiences with men bored her, and for several months she went through the public gestures of a lively affair with another young actress. Ernest could recall spending whole evenings trying to make Lee see that there was nothing real or worth while about Alice. He had been perfectly right. What now amazed him was his failure to see the plain implications of his rightness. The Alice she tried to palm off on you was bogus, not at all the actual Alice.

The situation, seen in retrospect, was of the simplest, most infantile, and obvious sort. Alice was intelligent enough to be aware of her failure as an actress. Ashamed and wounded, yet afraid to quarrel with the only friends she had made, like a child she hated them and hated herself. She would be desperately bad; if possible, hurt herself, and they would be sorry. Getting Lee, she was consoled, all was forgiven. She dropped the actress pretense. Having the person she wanted, she no longer needed to make other people notice her.

Ernest was resolved to try to stand her, for Lee's sake. He soon enough found it no effort. While not brilliant, Alice was shrewd, sensible, dependable. Her sense of humor was much livelier than Lee's; and so, too, was her sense of responsibility. Ernest did not know just when, but as time passed, he had completely reversed himself; begun quietly to put up with Lee for her sake, unable to imagine what she saw in Lee.

Kissing her, he said, "How well you look! And how smart!"

"And how freckled," Alice answered. Her light red hair was almost carrot colored, a pale shining orange. To match it, she had eyes of a light, rare brown. "Ernie, you're such a comfort, though you haven't the faintest idea what's smart and what isn't. You happen to be right this time; but I often wonder why it is that you have no taste outside architecture and music. You really haven't, you know. It must prove something."

"I have a cultivated and excellent taste in painting and sculpture, in literature, food, wine, and women. Besides, architecture and music are the only arts, anyway. The rest are just excuses for not earning an honest living. Come. I'm hungry. What's Lee up to?"

"Oh, they're going on the road with that damned play and he's all of a dither. He's started nursing his soul again, too. I don't know why I live with him, except that he gets less and less able to take care of himself. And then, of course, when we arrange a truce, he can always gratify my sensual nature immoderately."

Ernest smiled. "I'm not going to discuss your love life with you," he said. "You'd better tell me about Lee's soul. Or if he's going to be free later, I'll leave a message for him and he can come over and tell me himself."

"Don't bother. He and Meyer will simply sit around reminding each other how wonderful they are and getting drunk. I know Lee by this time. Late tonight he'll get in his great lover mood and want a woman. He's timid about such matters, so I'll be the woman. Tomorrow he'll be sick and sorry, and that's fine. But I wish he could omit the amorous stage—just be sick and sorry. It's bad enough to be his wife without having to double for his whore."

"I understand perfectly. Now, confine yourself to his soul." The doorman beckoned up a taxi.

Getting in, Alice said, "Oh, we met this Catholic priest on the boat. I think he said he was a Dominican or something. A Father McNamara. Good-grade smiling Irish. Fond of books and music. Very much up on the theater, of all things—"

"He's dispensed by the Prior Provincial," Ernest said with satisfaction. "The last time I saw him, he was even dispensed from Lenten abstinence so he could dine with the worldly without embarrassing them."

"Oh, do you know him?"

"Vincent? Of course I know him. At one time he was trying very hard to get me for the True Church. He's part of the great Dominican uplift which is going to make Rome socially acceptable here. For a couple of years now he's been avoiding me; I think, because I know his unfortunate secret."

"What on earth is it? He's not queer, or something, is he?"

"Lord, no! Worse than that. He's a convert. In fact, he started at the seminary with me. I remember that he used to keep a stoup of holy water in his room. He told everyone it was a real help in moments of temptation. It was quite a problem, getting genuine Episcopalian holy water, and I think it shook him. He never felt right at the seminary. He was charming, very learned and witty, and everyone liked him; but shanty Irish, just the same. His parents were probably born bog-trotters who made a fortune and then turned Episcopalian for social reasons. He came from the West, and there was a lot of that in the West—still is. The seminary happened to be running high and crazy and the first whiffs of incense started Vincent galloping home. I don't think it will do for Lee. It's one thing to like Vincent. But to like Rome, you really have to be born in it."

The taxi had been halted for two minutes in the tight traffic of a side street. Ernest could see a delicate sheen of sweat start through the dusting of powder on Alice's forehead and cheekbones. She stripped the white mesh gloves from her hands and flopped them a few times in front of her face. "It makes it worse," she sighed, letting them fall in her lap. "I'm not so sure about Lee. You know he's tried almost everything else. Yoga breathing exercises, and theosophy, and Christian Science. All sorts of things, really. We met some German nudists in Bavaria who worshiped Thor or Wodin or something. It was simply hysterical—it's too hot to tell you about it now, but I must sometime. If you could have seen this Hille Feike—he's the theater man—with his monstrous pot and rimless pince-nez! He said to me: 'Ilse, what pure lines you have.' I thought one was supposed to ignore all that; but, no. They compliment any newcomers in general and in particular, and some of the particulars! Even I blushed several times. But it's chaste. I expect, because everyone looks so revolting, and you're almost distracted with the insects and underbrush and no shoes. Lee got very serious about

Wodin and the Nordics. My God, how sick I am of him!"
Ernest laughed. "And how you worry about him."
"You're wrong, Ernie," she said, turning her head. "I
used to worry about him. I stopped that several years ago.
I worry about the trouble he makes me. He carries on so. I
think this Rome business is going to be serious."

"Well, it's not. People like Lee are Vincent's job, and
Vincent wouldn't still have it if he made many mistakes. It
isn't what Lee wants, but what Rome wants. Lee's prepa-
ration would take a year, and Lee would lose interest in a
week when they dropped the distinguished intellectual approach and got down to work. Just go into a Roman
church sometime—I don't mean one of the stops they've
fixed up for the carriage trade—and look at the congregation. Lee would find them rather common."

"Well, Lee's rather common, too, you know."

"I know. And that's just why he wouldn't be able to
bear them—or anything about it; because it's all common
as dirt."

"You're really the damnedest snob, Ernie. What would
Jesus say?"

"It's Lee who'd mind. My Chapel congregation isn't a
cut higher. In a church, Lee wouldn't have anything else
to do besides noticing that the man next to him smelled.
And you mustn't drag Our Lord into everything. It's a low
evangelical form of anthropomorphism. Instead, try wondering what the lightning coming out of the east, or what
the Incarnate Logos, would say. Here we get out."

The taxi drew away. Alice stood a moment on the pavement, looking at him. "The Incarnate Logos! Honestly,
Ernie, how do you keep a straight face?"

"Religion is another thing I don't discuss with you, my
dear. It is not meet to take the children's bread and cast it
to dogs." He grinned at her, striking her shoulder lightly

with his knuckles to drive her down the steps to the door. Inside, Joseph's shiny egg-shaped head appeared bobbing above his damp and stained dinner coat. "Just ten minutes, Mr. Cudlipp. I must allow for you to be late, sir."

"Quite right. There'll only be two of us. I think Mrs. Breen might like a cocktail."

"Heavens, no! I'm melting."

"I have a table for you up on the back porch, Mr. Cudlipp. There is a little more breeze than down in the garden."

"Good, good."

"You haven't heard the last of that dog crack, Ernie," Alice said as he seated her by the iron rail. "You can keep your children's bread. You'll never see this bitch sitting up begging, I can tell you. Still, if Lee has to go Christian, I can't see why you—"

"I wouldn't receive him. It's so long ago, you've forgotten; but I wouldn't, for the same reason that I wouldn't marry you two. You could get just as much married as you needed to be at City Hall—"

"I haven't forgotten. The reason you wouldn't marry us was that you were so furious at me for catching Lee—"

"I don't marry people who aren't communicants. I don't receive as communicants people who aren't Christians. I never have and I never will."

"Ernie, you're priceless!"

"Maybe so, my girl, but spiritual matters are a good deal beyond both you and Lee."

"You make me so mad, Ernie! I suppose that nobody can be spiritual who doesn't agree with you."

"Phrased that way, it is necessarily true," Ernest said. "It's a matter of definition, not of my opinion. Nobody is spiritual who doesn't in essentials agree with me. Just as nobody is a woman who doesn't in essentials resemble you.

You either have the capacity to apprehend the great spiritual truths, which are universal and invariable, or you haven't. If you haven't, they don't exist for you, any more than colors exist for a man born blind. You haven't. Now that subject is closed." He smiled at her steadily until her light brown eyes, glinting with annoyance, softened and she smiled back unwillingly.

"All right," she said. "I didn't want to talk about it anyway. It's just Lee's nonsense that got me started." She laid her hands, which had been clenched in her lap, open on the table. "So why don't we eat, darling?"

"Why not?" Ernest said. He peered over the rail, looking for Joseph. Below, the so-called garden—a double row of tables amid boxes and pots of poor trees and ragged vines—was open under the bare frame of awning canopy to the hot, clear, sunset sky. A few couples were seated here and there at the tables. Balancing through the twilight two glasses filled with pale cocktails on a small tray, a short fat waiter came quickly out. He swept them deftly down before the nearest couple, caught up the empty glasses, darted back.

"What is it?" Alice asked.

"Nothing. It's John."

"And who is John?"

"John Wade. He lives with me. I haven't seen him for a few days and I was getting worried about him."

"Do I know that name? What's he do?"

"Mainly that, I suspect—" Ernest bent his head a little toward the table below. "I don't know. I've gotten rather out of touch with him. He annoys me a good deal, because I'm beginning to think he isn't any good. For a long while I've thought he was. I had a good deal of influence with him—" He shrugged.

"Did I ever know him?"

"I wouldn't think so. He's twenty-two. Just before he

got out of college last year he won some sort of contest. Somebody paid him a thousand dollars for the best book of verse by an undergraduate. It was bad luck, because he already had about as much respect for himself as was healthy. He thought he wanted to go to France. When he came back in April, he was naturally broke, so I put him up."

Alice looked down. "I can't see his face, but I like his girl. I do know where I heard the name. It was called *Sun Poems*. Somebody sent Lee a copy."

"Yes, I know it made a moderate stir. There are so few people who read poetry, and so few critics competent to have an opinion about it—it's stopped being a natural or necessary means of expression. Nobody writing it has more than talent and it really requires genius. I don't think John's work—what I can read of it—is any worse than the best that's being written. It's just unnecessary."

"You're so positive about everything, Ernie. How do you know?"

"I can still read, my dear. I saw his book. It's very robust, and full of Indian names and American history, and infantile misconceptions about the character of pioneers, the nature of the frontier, and other optimistic claptrap—" He considered the back of John's head a moment. "Why on earth are we arguing? You're one of the few people I'm really fond of. Now, why aren't we having a wonderful time?"

"I am, Ernie. I swear I am. Do you remember how you used to hate me?"

"I do."

"I thought you were so marvelous."

"Did you?"

"And I still do. I love to hear you lay down the law. You make everything so clear and simple."

"That's what I mean to do. Ah, Joseph! It's about time."

A waiter brought over a serving table. Another rushed up with an ice bucket, whirling the bottle in it. "Open it, open it," Ernest said. "We haven't all night. I'll want to make a mustard dressing for the salad, Joseph. See that the cream is thin and the mustard German."

"Ernie, I won't have you dashing off somewhere. I'm not going home until I'm sure Lee has passed out, and I'm certainly not going to wander around town alone."

"I've an engagement at nine-thirty. I won't be long. I'll leave you at the Vicarage, and you wait, like a good girl. Oh, I forgot! You remember Lulu Merrick, don't you?"

"You mean—why, of course." She looked at him curiously. "I thought she must be dead."

"She's not. She's very likely to drop in. She seems to be in town."

"I'd like to see her again. Do you remember when she and Stella—"

"You won't know her," Ernest interrupted briefly. "Stella was committed. Did you hear?"

"Heavens, no! What was it?"

"A certain number of years of free drinks and what used to be called free love, mostly. You probably remember how amusing Lulu was about it being high time her daughter had a lover, and the steps she was taking to find a really competent one. I think Stella anticipated her, even so. If there's anything not to be doubted in this world, it's that he that soweth to his flesh shall of the flesh reap corruption. It's simple physiology, among other things—a form of God's truth. But none of them believes it until it happens to him—" He nodded down toward the garden again.

Dusk had definitely fallen. Strung from the ridge of the awning frame, electric bulbs inside colored paper lanterns had come on. At the tables where people sat, small lamps were lighted. Ernest could see the glow up the intent face and over the slight round bare arms and shoulders of the young woman with John. "John's a fine example." He lifted his glass, tasted the wine, and smacked his lips. "Johannisberger, I think," he said. "Joseph must have formed a high opinion of you." Below, the short fat waiter issued out from under the porch again, two glasses on his tray. He landed them with a precise flourish in front of John and the girl.

"Ernie," Alice said, "how do you manage to believe such rot? I keep forgetting you do; until you suddenly sound like my lamented father. He always talked that way —the way you'd expect a Methodist minister to talk. It wasn't any surprise, since he was unmistakably an imbecile."

"If some imbecile told you that two and two made four, would you feel that you had henceforth to believe that two and two really made five?"

She said, impatient, "I wouldn't feel that I had to believe anything. What seemed to me obviously true, I would treat as true. Do you mean that you think your John is being ruined because he probably wants to sleep with that nice kid, or because he plainly doesn't mind getting a little tight before dinner?"

"All right, Joseph, bring the salad. And pull over the serving table to put the bowl on. I can't hold it in my lap. Fine." He took up a wooden spoon, scooped a quantity of mustard into it. "I've known John for years," he said. "He used to turn up at some of the performances at Saint Matthew's."

"Well do I remember."

"Yes, it was wonderful fun; but it didn't get anywhere. I was a long time seeing that. Ogilvie doesn't see it yet. At any rate, John was a nice boy. I don't mean to let him grow into a despicable and disgusting old man without a struggle." He pinched up some salt and dropped it into the bowl of the big spoon. He took a halved lemon and squeezed the juice carefully. "This will be very good," he said. "In answer to your other questions, you ought to have better sense than to ask them. Drunkenness and fornication are in their nature wrong and the Church condemns them. As incidents, they aren't serious, they're simply stupid and mischievous. If you didn't romanticize them into 'getting a little tight' and 'sleeping with that nice kid,' you'd see their intrinsic dreariness."

"Well, I don't think either of them is wrong, and I never will."

"I'm not asking you to," Ernest said. "You may think they are as right as rain, if you like, and find you can. You're no part of my spiritual charge. Now, eat your salad. Didn't I tell you once not to talk about things you don't understand?"

Alice obeyed him meekly. She took up her fork and began to eat. After a while she said, "Ernie, I won't make you bother about me if you haven't time. I'll—"

"The bother's going to be yours. I want you to hold the Vicarage for me. The rector will probably be in. He's not a bad old boy, but curse and swear as little as possible in talking to him. He wouldn't know what to make of it. There's a bottle of extremely good brandy, which Martin Brooks gave me, in the dining-room cabinet—Lily will get you the key if you feel faint. But don't you dare offer a drop to Lulu if she turns up."

"I think I ought to divorce Lee and marry you, Ernie. I can see I'd really be very useful."

"You might; but I'm a celibate by conviction and inclination. Besides, if you were divorced, the Bishop wouldn't allow me to marry you. We had an uncomfortable case of

24

that kind in this diocese some years ago. I couldn't survive it. Because I was down at Saint Matthew's, my orthodoxy is already open to question. So put the idea aside."

"I don't think celibacy is healthy. Haven't you any normal appetites?"

"Appetites depend a good deal on what you spend your time thinking about. It's one of the practical principles of that spiritual life which you are incapable of understanding— Some ices, and you may bring the coffee with them, Joseph. Right away, please; I'm very late."

"Well, if I'm to be on duty all evening, I'd better retire to the ladies' room here for a few minutes. I expect it would be an occasion of grave scandal if I were for any reason found abovestairs in the dwelling of a celibate by conviction and inclination." She arose, laying her bag on the table.

"When you're in the mood," Ernest said, "almost everything you do or say might be occasion for grave scandal. But you can't possibly scandalize me, so why try?"

"Because I feel rather squalid tonight. By the pricking of my thumbs, something wicked this way comes. You wouldn't understand. You haven't the capacity." She wrinkled up her nose at him and disappeared inside.

The ices and coffee came on a tray carried by Joseph himself. He glanced quickly in the direction of Alice's disappearance, coughed, and said: "Mr. Cudlipp, could it be convenient for you to give me a little on account? Business is not good, or I would not ask you. And if it is not convenient—"

Ernest took out his pocketbook and inspected the contents. "You can have twenty-five dollars," he said. "I only have thirty. How much do I owe you?"

"About ninety-seven dollars, sir. Anything at all would be a great help to me. I would not ask it if—"

"I should hope not," Ernest said. He supposed that it was chagrin at the size of the amount that made him feel facetious. He said, "Don't take advantage of me. When I eat out, I have to eat here, because I can't find food fit to eat anywhere else. Now, be off, before my guest discovers my embarrassment."

Joseph obliged him with a flowery smile, and he added, "Don't give credit to Mr. Wade, if you're worried about money. He has none. It is all right to give me credit. It's only charitable. A man of my age must be careful about what he puts in his stomach; but Mr. Wade can as well as not eat at a lunch counter."

"Yes, sir. Thank you very much, sir. Mr. Wade told me I should put his check tonight on your account, sir."

"How many cocktails has he ordered?"

"I think, for both, eight, sir."

"You may put his food and two of them on my account. The other six you get cash for, or you will never get anything. Does Mr. Wade bring that young lady here often?"

"Several times, I know, sir. Not so often as he used to come with Mrs. Binney."

"Well, ponder the circumstance, Joseph."

Pondering the circumstance himself, Ernest could see that Geraldine must have done most of the paying. That wouldn't be likely to violate John's principles. Defiant, John frequently said that money was the only thing of any importance in the world. John was getting back with happy malevolence at the governors, teachers, spiritual pastors and masters who had taken advantage of his youth and inexperience to say that wisdom was better than rubies. Geraldine would quickly persuade him to be sensible about the money. "Tell Mr. Wade," he said to Joseph, "that I asked for him, that I particularly wanted to see him sometime this evening. But not until we're gone. I don't want to see him here, or in company."

26

Alice came out on the porch and he arose. "I'll pass up the ice," she said. Standing, she took the coffee cup and saucer, lifted the cup and emptied it. "It's twenty minutes after nine. Don't think you can hurry me over an appointment of yours and not hurry yourself. What is this mysterious appointment, anyway?"

"Oh, a young married woman who hasn't been using very good judgment. I imagine she wants to get something off her chest."

"Now, don't be rough on her, Ernie. With men what they are, being a woman is almost more than anyone can bear."

Ernest shook his head. "No, no! Don't give me that stuff! Save it for some other romanticist, like Lee. There's no reason to feel the least pity for women as such. They get on very well."

"Little you know!"

"Lots I know. Compassion is one thing. Sexual sentimentalism is something else—in fact, it's a tepid little aphrodisiac; the beauty-in-distress fantasy. Don't ask me to regard the disabilities of women with reverent awe. You haven't been female for all these years without knowing what nonsense it is."

"What do you mean, all these years?" she said. "And you damned well ought to be a woman for a while and see how you liked your Heavenly Father's rotten stupid arrangement for perpetuating the race."

"That's my good girl! Be mad; don't be quiet and brave. Come. We're off."

Under the white glow of the arc light before the Vicarage, Ernest helped her from the taxi. On the convenient, spacious steps of the Chapel adjoining, a group of boys sat or squatted in a close circle. There was a thin clatter of rolling dice, a chorus of exclamations, the ring of coins thrown down.

"Go on in," Ernest said, "the door's open. On the piano in the back room are the scores of some fine French carols Canon Cole sent me from Paris. Try them over."

He advanced directly on the group on the Chapel steps. "If you can afford to spend that money gambling," he said, "you don't need it very badly." There was a general starting back in consternation. "Fred," he said, recognizing one of the boys from his choir, "your friends may not know any better than to start a crap game here, but you do. Just pick up that money and I'll put it in the poor box for you."

"Nuts!" somebody said.

"Young man, I don't think you belong on this block. If I speak to Father Maloney about you, and he speaks to your parents, you won't like it. Now, beat it! All of you!"

———— • ————

Ernest returned to the taxi. "All right," he said. "Start uptown. I'll think of the address in a minute."

He propped his feet against the back of the folded-down seat in front of him, reclining with closed eyes to the light sway and jolt. For a moment he thought of Geraldine, and his impression of her was not full or clear. In May or early June she had been twice to dinner at the Vicarage. She had come down to a number of services—he could recall, in the course of more than one sermon, observing her with surprise seated in back with John. Her clothes—Alice was right; he didn't notice or know anything about women's clothes, really—were simple and severe. He ought to pay more attention, for he could see that there might be useful trifles of information in knowing how good or expensive they were, or how smart. It seemed to him that she had worn white to dinner; to church, a dark blue with some white at the throat. Or, very likely, she hadn't. That might be merely the general effect of whatever she had worn on his inattention. She was somewhat blonde, her hair more brown than yellow; her eyes dark, her nose short and straight. He hadn't thought of it before, but the person she resembled was Wilber Quinn. She shared, and in a way not especially feminine, Wilber's boyish, clean and well-groomed tone of skin and hair, his frank, direct expression, his air of amiable receptiveness, rather than intelligence. She would be good with children, competent and comforting.

Time enough to deal with Geraldine's difficulties when he found out what they really were! Ernest relaxed more in the shadows, consciously loosening each muscle, blanking his mind, focusing his eyes on the inside of his eyelids, forcing on himself a poised, vacant quiescence—the brain resting, and, for the time of a moment, disengaged, held still.

He made no voluntary movement. He thought of nothing. He could measure the inflow of physical refreshment like coolness in the night and he began with firm tranquillity to let his mind form words: *O send out thy light and thy truth that they may lead me, and bring me unto thy holy hill, and to thy dwelling.* Unhurried, the phrases occupied his whole mind. The words returned, of themselves, with unforced deliberation, over and over. Soon he was aware, without the distraction or the interruption of taking an interest in it, of the automatically increasing depth of his breathing, the modulation of his heart beat.

Set, by the familiar practice of his will, on the deceptive threshold over which some people stepped to a supposed spiritual apprehension—where the senses, starved of nervous energy, were narcotized, kept no more check on actuality; where reason, deprived of ideas to work with, abdicated, impotent; where Grace might very well appear,

29

as Calvin supposed, irresistible—Ernest released himself. Somewhat rested, he struck a match and lit a cigarette. The taxi driver said: "Far enough uptown?"

"How far are we?"

"Ninety-third Street."

"Too far. Go over and turn down Park Avenue. It's Eighty-first. I'll show you."

"I thought you was asleep."

"You thought wrong."

Ernest was reviewing as well as he could the shelves of books covering the walls of his bedroom in idle search of some likely source of light on John Calvin's personal religious experience. Nothing at all appeared to him. He used to have—and surely had still, since who on earth would borrow it?—an edition of the *Institutes of the Christian Religion* translated and laboriously annotated by an old-style Princeton Seminary supralapsarian—what a marvelous word, by the way! The Presbyterians, overturned in a doctrinal rout, with the liberals persecuting the conservatives, must now be altogether—didn't they call it, infralapsarian? Calvin would spit on them! They were no better than Lutherans. Genuine Calvinists, who didn't blench at a little sound logic, who really considered the fall of man inhumanly preordained by God's eternal decrees of reprobation, must have grown as rare as great auks. It might be interesting to try to determine the true nature of the changes—why the Calvinists had once accepted easily teaching so stern and awful; why now they were rushing to exchange it for a flaccid Arminianism, a mess of Methodist pottage.

His reflection was restless. Ernest recognized it, concerned; for ordinarily, presented with such a topic, he began to work with interest, gathering materials in his head, considering and classifying them in relation to each other until he had isolated the point or points he must look up sometime.

Brought to a pause, he glanced at his watch, struck his hand sharply to the side of his face. "Cudlipp," he said, "I think you are insane!" He started forward on the seat. "Quick!" he said to the taxi driver. "Get down to Eighty-first Street! I'm hours late! Go on! Turn over there—don't stop for the light—"

The taxi swerved on the corner, went roaring west. It darted south on the changed light, across the traffic starting north. Four blocks down they swung into Eighty-first Street and Ernest called, "Right there! Pull over!" He jumped onto the pavement. To a doorman in white linen he said, "Quick! Get in and ring Mrs. Roger Binney. The Reverend Mr. Cudlipp calling."

"Yes, sir."

"At once, at once, please!"

The taxi driver looked at them both, the doorman propelling himself across the wide pavement to the lighted alcove of the switchboard beyond the big doors; Ernest, standing alert and troubled, digging silver from his change pocket.

"So you think I'm crazy, do you?" Ernest said. "Sometimes I do myself; but I have a strong premonition. There you are. And there's fifty cents for getting here. Good night."

The elevator man had the switchboard phone to his ear. He and the doorman turned and stared at Ernest. "I didn't see Mrs. Binney go out, sir," the doorman said, "but she doesn't seem to be in."

"Is there a pass key? Get it. We'll go up."

The elevator man, gaping, closed his mouth suddenly, opened it again, and blurted in the mouthpiece: "Reverend Mr. Collins, Ma'am . . ."

"Cudlipp, Cudlipp," Ernest said. He stepped into the elevator, stood leaning against the wall. By his wrist watch he was hardly more than twenty minutes late; but only a simpleton would be late at all. The circumstances, considered with any intelligence, shouted it to him. Unless she was really desperate, a young woman like Mrs. Binney would never telephone him. Any idiot would have sense enough to know that. Only at her literal wit's end would she be able to make herself presume on an acquaintanceship altogether nominal. Her air of intimacy was unreal, no more than an imitation of John's intimacy.

"To your right, sir," the elevator man said.

In the hall, Ernest thrust his thumb against the bell button. The door immediately swung back. Unable to see, he walked forward through the dark entry toward a light beyond. Over his shoulder he said, "Don't ever think of doing that, Geraldine. Besides being vulgar and nasty, it wouldn't be forgiven you, either in this world, or in the next. There are too many people involved. How do you think they'd feel?"

The door clicked closed. "How do you think I feel?" she asked faintly.

He turned. "You know, it just suddenly came to me," he said. He laughed. "What you'd do, I mean. Not the sort of thing I'd expect from you." He put his hands hard on her shoulders, and held her while she wavered a little, regarding her steadily in the deep shadow. "You feel like hell," he said, "to the approximate degree of your aversion to God and your conversion to creatures. Go. Fix your hair. Wash your face. I don't want to see you this way."

He dug the fingers into her shoulders until, wincing, she tried to free herself. "That's better. You see, you easily can, if you want to. If you let go that way, I can't do anything with you. If you help me, I can do everything that needs to be done."

He released her and she put up a hand, rubbing her shoulder slowly. "No, you can't do anything," she said; but her voice was composed. "No one can do anything. I realize that. When I telephoned you I don't know what I thought. I'd just got in. It seemed so horrible—everything—that, well, I don't know. When you didn't come, I saw how silly I was—what could you do? What—"

"You're feeling better already," he answered. "Do as I say."

He went in toward the light. The living room was large, and looked even larger than it was, for it had almost no furniture—two chairs, a card table under the shaded glow of a floor lamp whose short cord stretched away taut to a baseboard plug. A handsome, heavy secretary desk had been pushed carelessly into a corner. The floor was bare, the quartered oak dusty, littered with small rubbish. The wide windows, open on the summer night, had neither curtains nor shades, only the empty brackets which must have suspended Venetian blinds. John had mentioned—or maybe she had—that she was moving. Probably she hadn't intended to be in town at all.

Ernest stood a moment at the windows, watching the city—the heavy dark masses, the far-flung direct lights of the great avenues, the indirect flares and glows. A breeze was perceptible up here, steady and persistent, but tepid. "We'll get a thunder storm," he said aloud.

He turned back. On the bridge table lay Geraldine's bag and hat, a pair of twisted white gloves, a bottle of sherry and a glass, a box of biscuits torn open. He picked up the bag thoughtfully, snapped the catches. Inside were a number of crumpled bills, a handkerchief, damp and soiled, a cigarette case in black enamel with small gold initials, a matching lighter; a compact, a lipstick, several keys; an envelope postmarked Cincinnati, addressed to Mrs. Roger Binney, 2nd; and, as he expected, a small straight glass vial with one dozen veronal tablets.

Ernest shook his head. What amazed you was the uniformity, the uncontrolled, not intentionally directed, but inevitable, sameness with which people proceeded to act out—though with real enough agony or desperation— the unreal, conventional emotional part. *When lovely woman stoops to folly*—the remedy, supposing of course that she knew she was stooping and could recognize folly, was classic. In a high-strung, ugly way, it was almost comic —at least, to the moment of swallowing the veronal. The veronal was as real as the anguish which had brought on the whole essential false and artificial gesture. It would re-deem—in the sense of make serious—both the folly that recommended it and the folly that swallowed it. It was entirely realistic and straightforward. He heard Geral-dine's footsteps coming through the empty apartment. Laying down the bag, he held the glass tube up. "I took the liberty of looking for this," he said. "At the moment, it isn't possible to treat you as a responsible person. Sit down and drink some of the sherry. Where did you get these tablets?"

"The man at the drug store told me I could buy them in New Jersey."

"He must be a man of very little sense. So you went to New Jersey and bought them! I don't like that, Geraldine. That's not impulsive, that's deliberate. Do you wonder that I can't treat you as a responsible person? How did you ever get yourself mixed up in anything like this? What's wrong with your husband?"

"There's nothing wrong with him. I can't stand him, that's all."

34

"That's never all. You must have been able to stand him when you decided to marry him. How long ago was that?"

"I don't know—well, seven years, about."

"How old are you?"

"Twenty-eight, or I will be next month."

"Then you weren't a child when you married. Now tell me what it is that makes you feel you can't stand him."

"I don't want to talk about him, Ernie. You'll have to believe that I can't, I really can't, stand him. He's repugnant to me. I can't live with him. I—"

"All right. We'll come back to that later. How about your children? Are you tired of them, too?"

"Ernie, how can you say such a thing to me? Can't you see that I'm almost crazy? Can't you—"

"I can see it, my dear. Now, I want to know about John. He's been sleeping with you, hasn't he?"

"Of course. Do you have to ask?"

"How else am I to know? You don't imagine it's a subject I'd discuss with John, do you?"

"I don't know," she said. "Sometimes I think anything's possible. I thought it was pretty obvious to you."

"It was. But in matters of this kind, Christian practice is to give people benefit of the doubt. However obvious it might be that you were infatuated with him, it might still be possible for you to feel some respect for your moral and social obligations."

"If you mean Roger, I don't feel any obligations toward him, Ernie. I never loved him. I—"

"Your obligations are toward yourself. You were the one who engaged yourself to abide by a contract as solemn as possible. If your word is good only so long as it is comfortable and agreeable for you to keep it, then clearly you have no regard for your obligations."

35

"Ernie, what's the use? I thought I wanted to marry Roger, of course. But how could I really know what I wanted? Hardly any men were interested in me. I'm not pretty and I never was. At Vassar I did my work, instead of going to dances and on weekends. I could have. I have a sister who's really attractive, and she quite often made people invite me. Only I didn't want to—" She fixed her eyes on him in desperation, as though he might doubt it. "I know it sounds as if I were miserable; but I was awfully happy. I didn't have time for all that. I was almost always on the honor list. I had lots of friends. I was treasurer of my class, and, oh, lots of things like that that sound silly now—" She had begun quietly to weep, her elbow on the table, her face bent against her wrist.

"Just so." Ernest lit the cigarette he had been turning between his fingers. "By temperament and training you were a nice girl."

She caught her breath spasmodically two or three times. "No, I wasn't," she said. "I don't think I was, really. I—"

"I didn't suggest that you were perfect. Doubtless you can remember failings in charity or chastity. It would be strange if you couldn't. You met John in Paris last year, didn't you? Was that the first time?"

"Yes."

"How did it happen?"

She took the handkerchief from the bag. "I went over with my sister. John had a place with her brother-in-law— quite a good deal younger than her husband. I mean, John's friend was the brother of my sister's husband—"

"Yes. I understand. Go on."

"Well, he and John had been at college together, and they had an apartment. They were both so sweet to us— we had such a lovely time. Going places and doing crazy things, I mean."

36

"But there was nothing between you and John then. You hadn't thought of such a thing. The four of you simply went dancing and drinking, and out to Chartres. And you all liked each other a lot."

"Yes. How did you know?"

"How could I help knowing?" Ernest asked patiently. "I know what you're like. I know what Paris is like. I lived there for some time after the war. There are several sorts of pretty well standardized American behavior. I've seen them all."

He leaned back in the chair, the cigarette smoking steadily in the corner of his lips, his eyes narrow and thoughtful. Allowing himself a moment's release from the disagreeable, overeasy task of badgering Geraldine, he nonetheless watched her gravely and steadily. As well as he could, he made himself see her freshly, for the first time; disassociated from John, or from any particulars of her history or character which came from meeting her previously and hearing her talk.

Certainly he knew what she was like. It was there to be seen, for everyone was in fact exactly what he looked like, provided that you had the experience to know what you saw. As he had said, she was a nice girl. Not in the casual trifling sense of a complimentary generalization; but deeply and definitely; in a way whose vitality and importance was nowadays generally overlooked or disparaged. She would represent well enough what he had to regard as the one convincing possibility of steadiness, of virtue and integrity, in the dissolving turmoil of an unlimited transition.

Her appearance advertised a breed or stock which, succeeding by its strength, was invigorated and encouraged by its success. Ernest didn't doubt that, finding all right with itself, it was too ready to find all right with the world; but at least no doubts hampered its initiative. It had nothing to live down. If, relatively, it had been fortunate; relatively, too, it had been superior in intelligence, in capability, in perseverance. No one had ever been in a position to humiliate it. The only contempt it faced was from people out of its sight, beyond its understanding, beneath its own contempt.

This seen, everything was seen—facts of her background and training spoke through her—her father would be perhaps a banker, locally trusted and respected in southern Ohio; or perhaps a doctor well known in Cincinnati; or a conservative, by his lights, earnestly just judge—something of the sort.

Born into a home perhaps architecturally tasteless, but comfortable and carefully maintained; sent to a simple sufficiently good school; nurtured in an entirely unemotional, fairly Low Church faith—old Bishop Vincent might have confirmed her; dispatched to a women's college in the East where not impossibly her mother had gone before her— Ernest sat up sharply.

"Geraldine," he said, "in my work I've had a great deal of experience with cheap people. I don't expect much of them. As far as I'm given grace to, I try to love them, since in God's sight they are precious. I do what I can for them. It isn't much, because there is usually little to work on." He leaned forward, pointing the cigarette at her. "Many of them seem to be simply bad stock, bad blood—just what those things really are doesn't matter. Whatever they are, I have seen what they mean. The matter is practical, not theoretical. They have no chance because they are no good. Why they are no good is another matter, not relevant at this point—" He drew a breath. "Just as they have what has been put in them, you have what has been put in you. You were born with almost every good thing. There is invested in you the hope and faith of a decent, dutiful people for a future of decency and duty. Take care of that! You've got the thing worth having, if only you won't throw it away before you find out what it is."

"Yes, I know," she said. "It sounds all right, Ernie; but it isn't like that. I can't think what I ought to, unless I do. It wasn't like that. I suppose you have to think that it was wrong when John seduced me. Only I know it wasn't. I knew it was all right for him to have me. I could feel it was all right—"

Ernest snapped the end of his cigarette out the open window. He rubbed the top of his head. "Lord help me," he said. "What can I do to make you use your intelligence? Well, first. You don't honestly imagine that John seduced you, do you? Can't you see the meaning of the things you've told me? You thought John was wonderful. What do you think John thought, except that you were a sensible girl to see it? You seduced him, of course."

She pressed the handkerchief to her eyes. "I didn't," she said. "How could you believe it? I suppose you think I'm so ugly and common that—"

Gazing at her, Ernest did not answer. She lowered the handkerchief at last. "I didn't," she repeated. "It happened because I couldn't stop him—" She colored a little. "I mean—"

"That's what you mean," Ernest said. "It doesn't need any change. Of course you couldn't, because you didn't want to stop him. I suppose you'd both been drinking— but even so, you'd have to let him see that it was a pushover before he'd make any serious advances. The only way it can be that is for you to want it to be."

"I didn't! I—"

"Of course you did, my dear. John isn't overwhelming. He's just a young man with an ordinary itch. Undoubtedly he liked you. As soon as he saw that he could have

39

you—you know you'd have to be definitely repulsive for him to pull up at that point."

"Ernie—" she said, strangled.

"My dear, how little we'd disagree, if you'd let yourself see things as they are—or were. Evil can't be done in a nice way. In violating your morals you'll certainly outrage your sensibilities. No, you're not ugly and common. That's why you won't look at it. This great-love business takes two. As far as John's concerned, you can see what it amounts to. He's sick of it. I daresay he has been for a long while. He couldn't have the experience to know what he was letting himself in for. I'm sure you've taught him a lot. Another time—"

She put both hands over her face, dropped her head down to the table. "Come, come!" Ernest said. "Sit up. I won't allow you to start that. You had your emotional spree this afternoon. I don't condemn you, Geraldine; but don't imagine I'm here to condole with you. I want you contrite, not bawling over lost candy. You don't mean to tell me that you don't know how John finally got out from under?"

She sat up; she brought her hands down. With her eyes still shut, she said, "I know. I just couldn't seem to believe it. I knew the last night he was up here. Oh, God, Ernie, it was so awful. I knew he wasn't just tight. He kept saying: 'This is terrible. This is terrible!' But he wouldn't tell me what. He'd say— Who is she? What's she like?"

"I don't know. I've only seen her once, at a distance."

"He hasn't been having an affair with her, has he? He couldn't be! He couldn't—"

Ernest sighed. "I don't know that he is; but of course he could. If he isn't, it's because she won't let him. You don't support the finer feelings long when you do without principles. He's a sentimentalist, so he probably finds it all

40

very sad and moving—and unpleasant. But he doesn't stop it. None of them does. That's enough of that. Worry about your own behavior, not his. Where are the children?"

"At my sister's."

"Telephone her and tell her you're coming there. I haven't any idea what the exact situation is with your husband. What does he think you've been doing—or does he know?"

"He's in Cincinnati. I told him I didn't think I was coming back to him, he'd have to let me alone while I—"

"Then write him. Tell him that now you think you are. If he will start again and try to make a go of it, you will."

"I can't."

"You can. Get out of this mess. Go back home and behave yourself. That's easy enough. There isn't anything here for you." He held up the vial of veronal. "When all you can think of is this, what do you call it? Peace and pleasure?"

"Ernie, I would if I could. Why don't you believe me? I can't!"

"Geraldine, what is this nonsense?" He looked at the veronal tablets a moment, speculative. "Haven't you been frank with me? I asked you what was wrong with your husband. When you answer, nothing, I assume that you are telling the truth. This isn't the moment for reticences of that kind. What is he? Habitually unfaithful? Diseased? Impotent? Perverted?"

"Oh," she said. "No! No!" She looked at him a moment, her eyes wide, blank and despairing. "I suppose I have to tell you," she said. "It seems so silly. You see, I couldn't, I really couldn't. Ernie, I'm a couple of months pregnant."

Ernest dropped his hands and looked back at her. "Geraldine," he said, shaking his head, "Geraldine. Why did you let that happen?"

"It's silly, isn't it? That's just what I did. I suppose I didn't care. I loved John. I—"

Ernest pressed his palms to his forehead, slid them up, over his thin brown hair. "Were you insane, my dear?" he asked. "I suppose you were! You didn't care. You loved John. And so you thought you'd have a child. Geraldine, a child is a human being. Merciful God, must I tell a sensible woman that? When you undertake to have one, you embark on a business of the greatest seriousness and importance, lasting perhaps twenty years. What on earth am I going to do with you?"

He found a new cigarette slowly, lit it, slouched back in the chair. He put a hand over his eyes and said, "I'll have to think. I'll have to think."

At last he said, "No. Definitely no!" He dropped his hand, crushed the barely begun cigarette out in the ashtray on the table. "Now, let me see what we can do. How about your sister? Would she know— Wait. We can do better than that. Where is the telephone?"

In the darkness of the entry he put his back to the wall. "Lily?" he said. "Mr. Cudlipp. I want to speak to Mrs. Breen, the lady upstairs. Tell her she can take it on that telephone in the back room."

There was a prolonged pause and Lily said suddenly: "She's playing on the piano, Mr. Cudlipp. She don't hear me."

"Now, Lily, go upstairs at once and make her hear you. If those stairs are getting too hard for you to climb, do you know what I'm going to have to do? I'm going to have to get a new housekeeper."

"I'm going, Mr. Cudlipp, as fast as I can—"

After a while a receiver clicked and Alice said, "Ernie, don't you dare tell me you can't get back."

"I'll be along. Listen carefully. Do you know of a decent and capable doctor who will take a case for me?"

"What kind of a case?"

"Try not to be dense, my dear. When I ask you for such information, what kind of a case would you imagine?"

"Oh! Yes. Of course, Ernie. I know a very good one."

"Well, please call him right away and make sure he's in town. I want an appointment for tomorrow."

"She, darling. She. I know she's in town. I was there this afternoon. Not the same thing, though. A funny old man put his head in while I was playing the piano, started to say something, and then ran away as fast as he could. Do you suppose he was a burglar?"

"I suppose he was Mr. Johnston. He's a clergyman who assists me."

"Oh. I'd thought he might be the janitor. Lily's more remarkable than ever, isn't she? I expect I'd fire her."

"She is an extremely good cook."

"Well, it wouldn't hurt her to dust some, sometime. Lee called up, fine and drunk. I think he wanted to apologize to you for missing dinner; but when he found it was I, all he did was accuse you of having designs on me. I told him no such luck and to go to hell. Good-by, darling."

Ernest went back into the bare living room. He took the veronal tablets from his pocket, broke the seal, and shook out two of them. "Do you ever take this stuff?" he asked.

Geraldine shook her head. He put one tablet back and laid the other on the table. "Take it now," he said, "and go to bed. Everything's arranged. I'll call you about it in the morning."

"All right. I don't like it, Ernie. I don't think I ought to do it. I know it's silly to feel that way, but—"

"You ought not to have to do it," he said, "if that is what you mean. You have no right to put yourself in a position where you can only choose between evils, instead of between good and evil. But you cannot continue in any course which involves persistent violation of the rights of others." He fixed his steady brown eyes on her and said, "Come here, Geraldine. You've got into this over your head; but we won't let you drown. Kneel down."

She came automatically, knelt awkwardly, her dress catching tight under her knees, and he put a hand on her shoulder to steady her.

When he had occasion to use one, the long Roman absolution came first to Ernest's mind. It was a relic of seminary days. Spikes like Vincent McNamara and Carl Willever naturally championed it—though there had been a prolonged, enjoyable squabble over the admissibility of the deprecatory form. Thoughtful, Ernest began: "May Almighty God have mercy—"

But it was, he decided, too thick, in view of what Rome would have to say about his directions to her. He turned it into the words of the Prayer Book: "—upon you," he continued, "pardon and deliver you from all your sins, confirm and strengthen you in all goodness, and bring you to everlasting life; through Jesus Christ our Lord . . .

"Swallow that tablet," he said.

She put it in her mouth, her face contracting bitterly, and gulped the sherry left in the glass.

"That will take care of you," he said. "Good night, my dear. You're all right. You will be all right."

As the bright, silent elevator car sank with them the operator prepared to examine Ernest thoroughly. His uniformed back was stiff and straight. His expressionless face he held front; but much practice had taught him a quick, covert system of side glances, letting him see without appearing to look.

Since Ernest was seeking to change his trend of thought, to put Geraldine out of mind, the little trick was all he needed. Catching by accident the boy's guarded turn of

44

eyeballs, Ernest's interest awoke. It animated his mind with that refreshing surprise and endless simple wonder which he could find in the contemplation of a human being— Who and what was he, really? What did he think, and why did he think it? What always remarkable chain of circumstances brought him here to run this particular elevator? What did he expect of life; how did he see himself; what satisfactions or hopes or ambitions justified his existence in his own eyes?

The boy's first interest had, of course, been in what 11B was up to now; but he had become aware of Ernest's unexpected attention. He whipped his eyes front again, abashed by a curiosity livelier, more penetrating, more alertly inquisitive than his own. Given a different situation, Ernest would have enjoyed putting him at ease, getting out of him the simpler facts of his life and experience; inviting his opinions, uncovering his ideas. What a person like this thought of Geraldine and her affairs would probably be, at least indirectly, instructive.

But, Ernest recognized with a sort of regret, finding out about that was clearly unthinkable. Besides—he recalled suddenly the broad, loutish, Irish face of the doorman—it was altogether too easy to guess the fruit of the staff's obsequious, unsleeping surveillance. Respectful smiles and deferential answers would have their ordinary, ugly reverse in lewd, surreptitious stares at Mrs. Binney's legs and body, in the winks traded regularly behind her back, in the obscene speculations, the long dirty discussions surely held about her down in the locker rooms—

"Ah, Geraldine," he said to himself, unwillingly back where he had begun, "how could you? How could you stoop to entertain these people?"

Ernest wagged his head, tightened his lips. He came out under the lighted awning, waved away the doorman who had raised his whistle to summon some favored taxi from the corner. He moved off, stepping quietly and quickly down the warm, airless street.

It would be twenty blocks, a mile or so, to the Vicarage. Although walking must make him, as usual, late, he thought: "I'd better walk some, let it wear off. I'm not fit for anything further at the moment."

The thought, phrased and pronounced, depressed him. What would become of him and of his work when he was obliged to measure out parsimoniously little driblets of energy, when he would have to think whether he would better do this, or save himself to do that? " ' 'Tis the god Hercules, whom Anthony lov'd, now leaves him—' " he said aloud. "Cudlipp," he continued, "why don't you face it? If you go on this way, you'll be knocked out entirely. For one thing, your stomach won't stand it. To your habitual gluttony, you will have to add an hour or so's sloth after meals. And that's final."

He turned into the lighted drug store at the corner, marched up to the soda fountain. The place was deserted and he rapped on the marble with a coin. A cadaverous young man came from the cubbyhole where prescriptions were prepared, heard without interest Ernest's request for bicarbonate and water, provided it impersonally.

Perched on a stool, Ernest sipped this disagreeable drink. Regarding himself in the great mirror that confronted him he realized that he must have left his hat somewhere— In the taxi? At Geraldine's? Ruffled by his bad habit of pressing his hands over it, his scanty hair was in confusion, a spare wispy tangle on his round head. The gray flannel suit made his cheeks and forehead look dark —liverish. Under his eyes he could observe a slight but definite dark pouching. The lids lay relaxed, the eyeballs seemed to start out, whites visible all around the intense,

46

small, darkly blazing irises—the effect was almost epileptic.

He stared coldly back at this reflection, his elbows on the counter, the glass empty, his thought traveling idly where it would on its uncontrolled sharp tangents. Since he looked sick, he thought of illness, and so, of death. Death he contemplated directly and stolidly, testing as well as he could his conviction that he did not fear it, feeling for any flicker of mental or physical recoil—*though after my skin worms destroy this body*. . . . But the revisers of the Prayer Book, he remembered, found that worm business a little too unpleasant, perhaps a little too Elizabethan. Back in 1901 they rephrased it. That reconstituted flesh of Job's had been just destroyed, no agency specified.

He smiled. Yet, for someone like Geraldine, whose deeper reactions would be altogether emotional, physically emotional, the revulsion would be enormous. The despair, the miseries of mind which could drive her to consider it would have to be, at least as she saw and felt them, enormous too, probably beyond his conception.

He thought of women in his own experience. He remembered the devotion and self-sacrifice of his mother, at once noble and transcendingly selfish. Since nothing was too much to do for him, she laid on him the intolerable moral burden of finding nothing too much to do for her. Though she had died when he had not been more than sixteen, no doubt she permanently marked his life and mind. He did not miss the part that fear of any second such subjection to a woman's affections must have played in forming his attitude toward all women. Even in the conviction that he should be a priest it probably had a share. It would make him ready for a rôle which separated him, slightly, at least, from encounters with women on or-

47

dinary, equal terms. The implications of his cloth were bound to turn the interest of a great majority.

Ernest sighed, breath hissing regretfully through his teeth. When these things he could remember ceased to be a punishment he would no doubt be in his dotage—senility's one real compensation must be its soothing impairment of memory, a kind of autumnal haze. In it a man might see himself as he was, his lost friends, his spent life, more favorably—lapses and chagrins obscured, pleasures and achievements, by a less exacting standard, good enough. Fifteen or twenty years didn't begin to serve for this reconciliation, and gladly now Ernest would have thought of something else.

The truth was that his psychological aversion to women —if it really existed—had never been sufficiently strong to outweigh his absorbing interest in people. For anyone with a taste for the vagaries of human behavior, the average woman offered more material than ten men in the mere hysterical origin of most of her motives and almost all her feelings. Fascinated, Ernest had found it safe to be on friendly, indeed, as years passed, on familiar and affectionate terms with a number of women. Overconfident, he early risked emotional entanglement with a few; and in one instance, surprised by a charm which he had misunderstood enough to think honest and unfeminine, more than that.

At the time he found no difficulty in resolving the moral aspects of it in his favor. Considering his perceptions and his strong, quite frank, opinions, that was reasonable. He did not quarrel with it. But, ah, those opinions! Merciful God, those perceptions! That had been after the war, when he came back from Paris to Saint Matthew's. Like Doctor Ogilvie, he had been passionately, priggishly, broad-minded and liberal. The most benighted conservatives could hardly have regarded him with so hot an intolerance as he felt for them.

In his conceit, moreover, he really considered this attitude his own. He had somehow been able to see himself sprung from the seminary fully formed in his views and beliefs. He knew about life. In France, where he had served as an assistant chaplain at Evacuation Hospital No. 9 he thought that he had learned about death. He would have said that, by a happy coincidence, he had looked for and found in Saint Matthew's and Doctor Ogilvie the opportunity he needed to work out his ideas. Of course, the truth had been—how often the contemptible, classic excuse is the truth!—that Doctor Ogilvie had found him empty. Doctor Ogilvie gave him of the tree; and he did duly eat.

Doctor Ogilvie, good earnest simple, met him mind to agile mind, personality to matured personality. Ernest was instantly overpowered. In a week he had been filled to the brim with Doctor Ogilvie's fine magnetic contempt for a religion of little rules as opposed to a religion of the Free Spirit. Doctor Ogilvie, his eyes flashing, swinging his mane of shabby gray hair, literally sweating in the heat of his feelings, poured himself out to everyone. He was too busy giving; and, in a way, too innocent and reproachless, to spend time wondering how people used what he rashly gave them.

This excuse, seen today, was not by any means perfect, however. Doctor Ogilvie was never handicapped by the need for consistency. He had more than once made arresting pronouncements about carnal love as a natural, good, and joyous thing, requiring no extra consecration from either church or state; but in practice he wouldn't have tolerated for a moment its expression in the life of his curate—or in his own life. His perfect rectitude and impeccable private morals had assuredly been investigated at the Bishop's direction with the very hope of finding that Doctor Ogilvie practiced some of the immoralities which, in the Bishop's opinion, he disgraced and scandalized the diocese by preaching. For Ernest it had been necessary to feel that there were things he understood better than Doctor Ogilvie. He had been reasonably careful to keep any wind of the affair from reaching the old boy.

It never did reach him, perhaps because it did not last long enough; perhaps because Doctor Ogilvie, seeing in Ernest so many things of his own which he had just put there, had taken him to his heart, would see and hear nothing against him. Soon he had turned over altogether the Sunday evening services, innocently called Vespers, to Ernest. Since the congregation at the height of his curate's effort sometimes numbered close to a thousand, whatever Ernest chose to do was demonstrably right.

Ernest's choice was expressing himself. Those who came regularly might expect absolutely anything by way of evening worship. On one occasion he could remember reading Stephen Phillips' *Marpessa* in place of a sermon—not that poor forgotten Stephen Phillips wasn't an improvement on most ordinary sermons. There were pieces as profane (though perhaps not so long) which he wouldn't be beyond reading from Saint Ambrose's pulpit if any good reason for making his congregation acquainted with them occurred to him. Only, good reason in those days—the stupefying calm arrogance with which he assumed that he had great spiritual truths galore, realized in his own experience and ready to correct and inspire his hearers, was a hard thing to have to remember—had been some artificial guff; a false nervous exaltation of mind grown from the successful efforts to endow his own then current affair with spiritual values—in effect, ones like those which he had just finished chiding Geraldine for attempting to maintain around her adultery with John. Only worse, being more fluent and much fancier.

He saw the clock then, arose violently to his feet, rapping with the coin. The cadaverous youth came out, annoyed, slowly found him three packages of cigarettes. Looking at this curious person, Ernest hovered a moment, wondering if he had been the one who was so helpful about the veronal; and if so, why—not any ordinary impulse to be obliging, surely.

He put his hand in his pocket, took out the tube of tablets, dropped it on the counter. "There's something you might have use for," he said. "It comes from New Jersey."

Picking up the packages of cigarettes, he went out the door. Snapping his fingers at a taxi—he couldn't possibly take time to walk now—he tumbled in while it was still moving up, fell back on the seat, and called out the address of the Vicarage.

———— • ————

At the top of the weather-pocked sandstone steps the Vicarage doors stood open on the stifling night. Hung high inside, a lantern, alternately red and blue paned, in an iron frame twisted to scrolls and curlicues, dropped wan light on the worn, cracked, and not very clean marbled paving of a tight vestibule. Ernest's eyes met it as he mounted the steps. For perhaps the thousandth time, he thought: "I must have that unspeakable object removed!"

In the constricted hall, crowded by the long steep incline of the heavily railed stairs, he glanced through the arched double doors into the front room. A light burned there, but no one was waiting. Over the marble mantel of the fireplace hung a big, startling portrait of himself ten years ago, in a plain black cassock coming to his throat, a dully-showing large silver crucifix on the black wall behind his head, a little black prayer book in his stiffly done hands. Wanda Willett was dead now—a sad, silly life embittered by fruitless faith that her slight talent for painting was genius; a sad, ugly death, unnoticed for a month in a country shack, with her numerous, extravagantly cherished dogs, shut in the kitchen, all dead too—starved. Ernest had gone up and read a burial service which no one attended but the undertaker.

The sliding doors to the back room were closed. Through them came the ripple of the piano and Alice's voice, negligent and throaty: ". . . Car la guenon, le poison, elle est m . . . o-o-ort-e!"

Ernest grinned, crossed to the doors and parted them. "That's not suitable music," he said.

Alice let her hands pause on the keys. "Hello, darling. I thought it would be a nice change for the piano."

A liqueur glass of brandy stood at the end of the keyboard. She took it, wet her lips with it, and put it back. "I've almost expired of boredom. Harriet will see your girl at eleven tomorrow, before I forget. If you're the author of her shame, don't tell me. I couldn't bear it—" She tapped the keys into an easy lilt: "He left me for a damsel dark, damsel dark—"

"That remark wasn't very witty," Ernest said. "In fact, it was stupid and offensive. Get away from there." He pushed her shoulder, forcing her to rise, and sat down on the bench himself. "Let me see if you are still able to sing anything fit to sing."

She rested her fingertips on his back. "No, I can't," she said. "Ernie, you play so badly! What on earth is it? 'Where'er You Roam'?"

"That's right," he said, looking up at her. "Come on, come on."

"I can't! It's too high for me."

"Nonsense. If anything, it's too low for me." He began to sing.

"That's because you're simply miles off, darling. Stop it! Anyway, I'm not stupid and offensive. I was just joking. Don't you even know when I'm joking?"

"I know. And when you're stupid and offensive, I don't like it— Yes," he shouted. "Come!"

The door into the back hall half opened. "Oh, Munson," Ernest said, peering over his shoulder. "Come in. I need you badly."

"I'm sorry, sir. I thought you were alone. I haven't a coat on."

"Mrs. Breen will excuse you. Alice, this is Mr. Munson, my organist. And a fine one, too. Were you going to the corner for a glass of beer?"

Munson blushed. "Well, I'd thought of it, sir; but—"

"Is Lily still up? There ought to be beer on ice downstairs. You can have it here. Mrs. Breen needs an accompanist."

Blushing more, Munson came from the shadow of the doorway. "I'm afraid I'll be very ragged," he said. "I don't do as much piano work as I ought to." His narrow, pointed face and thin sharp nose remained rosy. He glanced at Alice, and then away. Then involuntarily he looked back once more at her shining light red hair, as though to confirm what his confusion had hardly let him see. He sat down on the bench. Being so close to her, he seemed unnerved—visibly made aware of the scent she used. He examined his stringy, powerful hands a moment, remembered that he had no music, and no idea of what he was to play.

Alice said, "If you're to be dragooned into this, Mr. Munson, we'll try to do things you like."

Ernest smiled, seeing how the slight tribute of Munson's

53

confusion heartened her. Her charm acknowledged, the naïve feminine transformation took place. Alice became at once more charming—a definite, deliberate sweetness. "I think," Munson said, rising in agitation, "I'll get some music. What do you sing?"

"Mezzo, as far as I can. I'm not at all good, you know. Your pastor is trying to scare you to death. Get anything you like."

Munson ran out, went pounding upstairs.

"Ernie," said Alice, pleased, "the boy is suffering the tortures of the damned. When you know he's so shy, what do you make him come in for?"

"For you. Don't you like him?"

"I think he's sweet. But all those blushes!"

"They're to show he thinks you're sweet. And so do I, my dear; and so do I."

"No, you don't. You think I'm stupid and offensive. But I'm sure he doesn't want to play."

"Of course he wants to play. I think possibly some girl he liked snubbed him awhile ago, and he believes, as a result, that he's unnaturally homely and not attractive to women. But he knows that he plays well. It's one way he's sure to show to advantage."

"He isn't very beautiful," Alice admitted. "But, then, I don't think I ever saw a really beautiful man—except Lee, ten years ago. And what a sell that was! Why don't you go down and get him some beer? It's so hot, I'd drink a little myself. It shows you can never tell about people. I wouldn't have supposed beer was one of his passions."

"It isn't. He doesn't like it very much. He just drinks it to please me."

"To please you!" said Alice. "What an extraordinary way for you to obtain pleasure, if I may say so."

"Oh, he knows I don't approve of pious young laymen,

54

and by training and instinct he's very pious. He wanted to do something rather worldly to reassure me. Of course it means I've reached the Old Fool stage—the bright young people resign themselves to humoring you. I did it to Doctor Ogilvie for years. Now I know how he must have felt when I was being so patient and adroit—"

"Wait, wait!" Alice said. "Just a moment. Did I hear you say that you don't approve of pious people?"

"I suppose you think you did," Ernest said. "But you didn't. Piety can be a serious and beautiful thing. And about what I did say, there's nothing out of the way. I'm an experienced clergyman, and you don't find experienced clergymen enthusiastic over pious youths. Our sinful nature isn't as simple a matter as that. When it seems to be, you're safe in treating it as a form of frustration, an unwholesome attempt to get out of wrestling with your angel. In twenty years I've seen two, possibly, three, exceptions."

The third might be Wilber Quinn. Wilber enjoyed the buoyant, optimistic insensibility of the so-called sound mind in a strong and healthy body. He was handsome; full of energy, good spirits, and religion. But Wilber's special, sustaining interests were in such not-exactly-devotional activities as the Church League for Industrial Democracy, and the seminary's Guild for Christian Social Action. At the same time he was getting into the Oxford Group business. Flushing a little he had faced Ernest's chiding resolutely. "They may do funny things, sir," he said—the Groupers were accustomed to disarm some of their critics by cheerfully agreeing with them; they did not mind being teased for Christ's sake—"but I know this. They're making Our Lord real to many people who couldn't be reached any other way. A lot of our stuffed surplices"—that was a good example of his simple, harmless humor—"are scandalized by our bad taste; but so they were in John Wesley's day; and the Church can thank them for the loss of eleven million Methodists who ought to be communicants of ours."

Wilber being Wilber, it had not seemed worth while to comment on any of the numerous errors in fact and analogy thus stated or implied.

"All right," Ernest said, "you go and play with them. But don't let me hear of you standing up and sharing your discovery of Jesus after years of sin, or you'll be all through at Saint Ambrose's."

For a while it had looked as though Wilber, affronted, would feel obliged to be all through. But soon he relaxed enough to chaff Ernest on his hide-bound attitude. He hinted playfully that the next Chapel entertainment would be an auto-da-fé. His cheerful manly voice continued to echo over men's club meetings while he told them that Our Lord was a worker, too; born and brought up in a working-class family.

Wilber seemed to be really a case of arrested development—one of the little children suffered with no other qualification to come to Jesus. Of course, Ernest reflected, you had to be a child, at least mentally, to feel the appeal of Doctor Buchman and the Groupers. What adult could accept as real and true that fairy-tale world in which their Dutch baronesses, Masters of Fox Hounds, and formerly intemperate butlers all walked laughing and prattling, the children of light, and the children of the day? No, Wilber wasn't actually pious—that was an adolescent stage, and spiritually Wilber wasn't as old as that yet. Very likely he never would be.

"Only two," Ernest corrected himself, "only two exceptions. I'll see about the beer."

A pitch-dark narrow hall, into which the stairs descended, ran past the dining room to an inconvenient service door under the front steps. The wide shabby kitchen at the back was paved in worn brick. It had three screened windows and a door on the little weedy pen of a backyard. A bare bulb, dangling from a wire over the table, was the only light on. Except for two soiled white cats the room was deserted. The cats were watching with a patience saints might envy what was plainly a mousehole in the corner. They ignored Ernest.

He opened the icebox. Half a dozen bottles of beer were crammed above, under, and all around the lumps of ice. Lily had the ice itself covered with pieces of sodden newspaper, for it was impossible to persuade her that the function of ice was to melt. Ernest pulled out the papers gingerly and flung them dripping into the sink. From the backyard arose a wail. "Don't you go throwing out my papers, Mr. Cudlipp," Lily called. "In that old box we couldn't keep ice one hour without them."

"Then we'll have ice delivered every hour," Ernest answered. "We will not have any more papers in the box. What are you doing out there?"

"I'm sitting for the air."

"Well, come in and cut up some cheese for me. Find some pretzels and a bottle opener. Did Mr. Quinn call?"

"Yes, he called."

With elaborate loud sighs and groans, Lily shuffled on the flagstones behind, opened the door, and tottered in. "He say he'd be by about eleven. He had to go to a meeting."

"Did you tell him what I told you to?"

"What did you tell me to tell him? You didn't tell me anything to tell him."

Ernest groaned. "Can't I trust you any more, Lily?"

"I do everything you tell me, Mr. Cudlipp. You didn't tell me—"

"Yes, I did. I don't know what I'm going to do with you.

Now, hurry up with those things. Did anyone else call?"

"Some. I wrote down some. I gave that Mr. Johnston them to put in your room. He looked for you. Run up and down stairs all the evening."

"Lily, Mr. Johnston is not your messenger boy. It's very impertinent of you to ask him to do things you ought to do yourself."

"Well, he was down here, and he was going back, and those stairs tax me when I work my fingers to the bone all day."

"Yes, I know how much work you do. Hurry up. Find a tray." She looked so wizened and forlorn, her small black monkey-face shining dolefully, that he added, "And I'll give you some money to get a little ice cream."

She brightened immediately into energy. "You're just an old fake, Lily," he said. "I ought to take a stick to you." He dropped a quarter on the table.

Mounting the stairs with the crowded tray, he heard her shuffling cautiously into the dark hall below him. With great stealth she took off the telephone receiver, uncertainly dialed a number. Pausing a moment at the top, Ernest heard her croak guardedly: "Bell Pharmacy? You send me up right away fifteen cents' worth chocolate ice—"

He pushed the door open with his foot. It encountered sudden, unexpected opposition, then swung all the way, disclosed Mr. Johnston clasping his bumped elbow.

"Oh, I beg your pardon, Vicar," he said. "I shouldn't have been in the way! I—ah—just wanted to—this lady kindly asked me to wait. But I won't think of troubling you now."

"You aren't troubling me." Ernest set down the tray. "This is Mrs. Breen, an old and very dear friend of mine, just back from Europe. Munson's bringing some music and she's going to sing. Stay. Sit down. Have some beer."

"Oh, thank you very much," Mr. Johnston stammered. His eyes winked, greatly magnified behind the strong glasses. "But I never indulge, Vicar." He began shaking with disjointed confusion. "Not that I—not that it's any matter of principle. No, no. 'Drink no longer water, but use a little wine for thy stomach's sake and thine often infirmities.' No. No. I find personally that I'm better without it—"

Alice had turned on the piano bench. She sat frozen, her eyes fixed on Mr. Johnston in an instant of amazement, shocked, almost frightened. She moistened her lips, clasped her hands together and said: "Oh, but do stay, Mr. Johnston."

"Thank you, thank you," he said. The deep creased wrinkles of his face reddened on the ridges. "For a few minutes, then. I greatly enjoy music."

He fumbled about, aimless, for a chair, the muscles of his throat twitching behind the sagging curve of the too-large clerical collar. Seated, he swung one leg over the other, wagging the foot up and down. Quickly he shifted it to the floor again, rubbing his big bony hands together.

Alice said, sitting rigid, "Tell me something you like, Mr. Johnston. If I'm able to, I'd be very glad to sing it."

"Oh, no, no," he said, swinging the leg back over his knee. "No, no. Don't think of it. I like anything. All music, all music—ah—" He was suddenly checked, as though he thought that he had appeared unappreciative, or ungracious. "Ah—a piece I much enjoy is 'There's a Long, Long Trail Awinding—'" He looked at her anxiously.

Alice moistened her lips again. "Of course," she said. She swept her skirt around and faced the piano.

For one practically untrained, Alice's voice was good. It was fresh rather than clear, without professional precision, but in a limited range, simply and naturally true. It was

59

the sort of voice that would attract any musician's attention, and then at once lose it; for Alice had passed the age when promising parts really have promise. In fact, Ernest thought that it had undoubtedly gone off a little since he last heard it. But, of course, with music like that—

Mr. Johnston said, "Beautiful, beautiful!"

The degree to which he had been moved must embarrass, make ashamed, anyone who saw him. "What a beautiful, beautiful voice," he repeated, swallowing. He had taken off his glasses. His red-rimmed, pale blue eyes were actually wet.

Ernest uncapped a beer bottle. Alice had remained facing the piano. She would be saying to herself: "How terrible! How terrible! I can't stand it!" A visible quiver moved her shoulders.

Ernest turned and called through the open door: "Munson, bring down your music for that hymn."

"Yes," said Mr. Johnston, recovering himself a little, "it brings back memories of the war years. I was in Canada for some months, and I well remember the Canadian troop trains. So many of those brave boys never came back."

"Give me some beer, Ernie," Alice said. "I'm frightfully thirsty."

Ernest tilted the open bottle. "Munson's done a good thing for 'The Bermudas'—that poem of Andrew Marvell's," he said. "You know: 'Thus sung they in the English boat, a holy and a cheerful note: and all the way, to guide their chime, with falling oars they kept the time.' We'll use it for Thanksgiving Day in a special arrangement for men's voices—a bass soloist and chorus."

"Coming, sir," Munson called. "I couldn't find—"

Muffled downstairs, a bell rang.

"That's the front door," Ernest said. "I expect it's the

60

rector. You'll have to excuse me for a few minutes. Go on and sing. It won't bother us."

In the hall he met Munson, hurrying. The delay, it was apparent, had been to let him put on a coat and necktie. "Do your hymn for Mrs. Breen," Ernest said, amused. "I'll be back presently." He went past him to the front door.

On the landing at the top of the sandstone steps Doctor Lamb stood, hat in hand, face turned to the obscure sultry sky, frowning. His straight figure, with the street light falling on him from behind, and the light of the vestibule lantern reaching him in front, had an arresting air of elegance. This elegance of Doctor Lamb's never ceased to be arresting. Eyes lingered on him with pleasure and a vague surprise, baffled. Soon you realized that his good appearance was due in part at least to his clothes. Not many clergymen could afford a first-class tailor. You grew unconsciously used to a ready-made quality, inexpensive and unbecoming, in what they wore. Given the finest materials and perfect fitting, clerical garb became positively novel— a dress of unsuspected grace and distinction.

Of course, Doctor Lamb in face and figure met his tailor half way. His gray hair was cropped, shaven almost monastically to a severe silvering on the sides and back of his shapely skull. His face was finely formed, too. In profile, forehead and moderate aquiline nose showed the perfect noble definition of an eighteenth-century medallion. His somewhat ruddy skin stretched ascetically close to the clean-molded bones.

This whole effect of glacial, genuinely aristocratic dignity, carried further by eyes of a fine frosty blue, had no special foundation. Doctor Lamb came of plain, far-from-consequential people—his father, he once told Ernest, had been a locomotive engineer. In much the same way, that arrogance or anger, of which he looked so frigidly capable, was in fact controlled and tempered by a nature courteous and amiable. His wish, and better, his gift, was smoothing things over, reconciling conflicting interests, preserving decent harmony—even, his relatively few enemies declared, at any expense of principle.

Doctor Lamb could be mulish when provoked; but, ironically, to provoke him it took nothing less than the rude and obstinate refusal to compromise. He had no patience with people who demanded extreme measures or drastic stands. The making of concessions he regarded as a part of charity and a proof of good faith and will. He would make them himself to anyone whose position of difference seemed to him morally tenable.

If some sacrifice of principle became, in the process, necessary, it was true that it would not unduly disturb him. As one gentleman to another, he was confident of mutual understanding with his Creator about the nature and means of forwarding, God in His great way, Doctor Lamb in his little one, the work to which they were both sincerely devoted. He was really, Ernest thought with respect and some affection, admirable. Resolved not to find him annoying, too, Ernest said: "Good evening, sir. Come in."

Doctor Lamb looked down from the sky.

"Ah, Cudlipp!" he said. "I'm very sorry to be late. I hope I'm not inconveniencing you? I won't keep you long." He looked at the sky again. "Dear me, I think it's going to storm. I just sent Albert home with the car. Very stupid of me."

Preoccupied, he preceded Ernest into the drawing room, accepted a cigarette. They sat down looking at each other and Doctor Lamb cleared his throat. "Cudlipp," he said, "I'm going to have to ask your indulgence. This is altogether my fault. It doesn't excuse me, but in explanation, I can say that I simply hadn't thought the matter out.

As you know, I was upset over details of the Centennial Endowment Fund—as I've told you, I don't think that any such fund is necessary or appropriate. It seems ungracious in the face of the Vestry's generosity, but I'm not happy about it. However, that's not the point. What I mean to say is that I spoke on the impulse of my own inclination. I approved of the idea. I still approve of it. By all means let the members of the congregation hear what their neighbors, who go to other churches, believe or are supposed to believe! It makes for better understanding. So far, so good. But, of course, in asking these ministers to speak in the Chapel, we're assuming that we have the Bishop's permission. Certainly this may be assumed in the cases of the Lutheran pastor, and Mr. Jones, the Methodist man. But—"
He broke off.

In the back room Munson had been playing quietly over the air of his piece. He raised the key and repeated it. Alice's voice, suddenly lifted, was quite clear: "Where the remote Bermudas ride, In the ocean's bosom unespied. . . ."

Doctor Lamb gave the closed doors a quick, astonished glance.

"Does it bother you?" Ernest asked.

"Not at all. I was taken by surprise. Well, what I intended to say was that in this case it would certainly be disingenuous of us to assume any such thing. Personally, I think it's right and logical, if you have the others, to have Rabbi Slesinger, too. But, Cudlipp, you cannot get around Canon Twenty-three! Even the Bishop couldn't. He's specifically authorized to permit Christian men, *Christian men,* to speak on special occasions, and so on." He cleared his throat. "I think a point might be stretched for a Unitarian, if there happened to be a Unitarian church in the vicinity. But a rabbi! My dear fellow, how can it be done?

The last thing the rabbi himself would wish to be considered is a Christian man!"

"I felt that it could be done," Ernest said. "I think the phrasing of the canon is inadvertent. The plain intention is to permit edifying talks by outsiders, and to forbid only what is irreligious or irrelevant. Obviously the term should have been godly men. I had to tell Rabbi Slesinger that, because of the technicality, I wasn't able to offer him the pulpit, nor even to seat him in the chancel. If the Bishop wants to split hairs, I felt that we might split some back."

"Then you've definitely invited him? But, of course, of course! You had every right to feel that you could count on my meaning what I said. How disagreeable and unfortunate! What on earth shall we do? We mustn't let any ill-feeling result."

"One thing we might do is leave the responsibility to me," Ernest said. "I'd risk it, if you were willing."

Doctor Lamb shifted in his chair. "No," he said. "No. Since I know of it, I couldn't properly allow that. And, more, I wouldn't at all want to, even if I could. It would be the greatest disservice to you, personally. Believe me. But I don't have to tell you that you aren't in favor at the Synod House. The Bishop never forgets, and never, to my knowledge, forgives. Make no mistake, Cudlipp. That's a very efficient office up there. Don't imagine they haven't kept track of you. Give them something concrete and they'll have you up before a Trial Board. That's not a good place for anyone who was ever associated with Doctor Ogilvie. You know that."

"Naturally I'd be prepared to face the consequences. I don't see how they could be very serious."

"No, no," Doctor Lamb said, "you'd find yourself entirely unprepared. That would only be the nominal charge. Perhaps you don't realize how vulnerable you are, Cudlipp." He shook his head vigorously. "Given one open and shut violation of a canon, they would be in a position to make other charges. 'From public rumor or otherwise.' I don't know whether you've ever troubled to read the constitution of this diocese. That's all the Bishop needs." He frowned. "I think they'd try to make it Conduct Unbecoming to a Clergyman. Remember the Bishop himself is entitled to nominate all the members of the Board. Your only right is to pick from the names supplied you those which you would prefer. Do you think you'd be given any choice worth making?"

"I don't see how it could get as far as a presentment," Ernest said.

Doctor Lamb gazed at the toes of his slim, neat shoes. "My dear fellow," he said, "many people who aren't personally acquainted with you regard you as something of an Original. There's an air about you, Cudlipp, which easily creates comment. Then, of course, the Saint Matthew's business! Wholly sincere people assured me when you first came here that you weren't a Christian at all. There were suggestions, perhaps not so sincere, of even more unpleasant sorts. I've had my hands full, on occasion."

"Do you want me to resign?" Ernest asked.

"Nothing of the sort! I simply don't want you to attract official attention, to set yourself up to be shot at by people who don't approve of you. As matters now are, you're quite safe. The Bishop won't go out of his way to quarrel with me while I'm rector of a parish like Holy Innocents'. He had all he wanted of that with Saint Matthew's, as you well know. And, Cudlipp"—he reached forward and tapped Ernest on the knee—"you must not open yourself to disciplinary action! In the future, if events move as I have reason to think they are, God willing, going to move, it might be a source of real embarrassment to me if you had anything like that against you. This isn't the moment to say more. You understand me?"

"Quite, thank you."

"Don't thank me. To do anything else would be to do less than my plain duty. I'm aware that you and I don't see eye to eye on minor points; but I believe that Our Lord works in and through you. The Church hasn't so many men of parts that we can afford to waste them. And the sad thing is, we aren't attracting the young ones we should, either. A state of affairs really very grave. I don't think its importance is— Well, it's sufficient to say that if and when I find myself in a position to, you may be certain whatever influence I have will be used on your behalf. In this diocese you have no future, Cudlipp; none! Thanks to the willful prejudice— There! Of course I'm prejudiced myself!" He leaned forward a little. "Candidly, I detest the fellow! He seems to me a snobbish, obnoxious, mean-spirited little bigot; and I cannot believe that his useful and remarkable talent for raising money altogether compensates for harm done in fields which ought to be more important to us. But he is the Bishop of this Diocese, and it's very wrong of me to speak that way. I wouldn't do it to anyone else. And, of course, we must defer to him as long as we're under his jurisdiction. You see that."

"I see it," Ernest said.

"Good. Well, about this present difficulty. Would you like me to write to Rabbi Slesinger? Or, I'll call on him, if you wish. Perhaps that would be better. I would want to be particularly sure that he couldn't suspect any form of— er—prejudice playing a part. Feeling on that point will crop up in the most astonishing ways, you know. In short, I'll do anything in my power to get you out of the trouble I've got you into. You do agree with me that it's not worth it?"

"I'm not in a position to disagree with you, Doctor. It's your parish. I could wish that Mr. Hurst had less influence with you." As soon as he had said it, Ernest was sorry. It was no more or less than the outburst of an irritation, petty and spiteful, somehow rising against all intention and reason at the fine display of Doctor Lamb's talent for avoiding unpleasantness. The inherent, unkillable small worm of human malice writhed; for, exasperatingly, Doctor Lamb could not only create his senseless little difficulty, but do it in such a way as to make you like him for it. His agreeableness, his consideration, his sincere compliments—even the disarming touch of temper about the Bishop—made him invulnerable. There was no reason left for the resentment with which a man defeated may expect to inspirit and solace himself.

"I'm sorry I said that, Doctor," Ernest continued at once. "It wasn't justified. Although it meant quite a lot of bother for him, Rabbi Slesinger was most pleasant and cordial, and I—"

Doctor Lamb put a hand on Ernest's knee. "My dear fellow," he said, "you have reason to be put out with me. And as for your remark, it was pertinent. Our ecclesiastical polity is at fault. It shouldn't be possible for the Senior Warden to forget, as on occasion he does, what I can only call his place. But while it's true that he pointed this out to me, he's right, Cudlipp. He often is. I try to keep that in mind." He paused. "Well, make your decision about the best approach to Rabbi Slesinger and let me know. We'll do exactly as you wish—"

Concluding, Doctor Lamb was, however, not quite finished. That was plain, for he sat still, looking at Ernest with wordless, sympathetic attention, as though to satisfy himself that the damage had been repaired; and to note with innocent content what a good job it was.

"Come to dinner next week," he said. "My wife's had to

go back to Greenacres. She's having a rock garden built. I'm all alone and we can have a good talk. Oh, by the way, Mrs. Darrow told me this evening that she wanted to give the mosaic for the apse. Glendale's got hold of a young German who really seems to have mastered the old technique. I'll send the designs over to you in a day or so. What he does is said to be indistinguishable from the work at Monreale—"

He stood up, holding out his hand; but, on the instant, the long drapes drawn together across the front windows swung with a soft sound, lifting out into the room. Stiff warm blasts of air came under them. Thunder banged in a reiterated dull rumble. Through the whole house, doors slammed, things fell over, on the rush of wind. In the basement Lily yelled dimly, "Mr. Cudlipp, Mr. Cudlipp, I think the window's open—"

In the back room the piano broke off. Munson called from the hall, "I'll close them, sir."

"And as for me, I'll close the door," said a new voice.

Wilber Quinn's robust face, shining with a few drops of rain above his turned-up coat collar, appeared where the light fell into the hall. "Oh, sorry, Vicar," he said. "Good evening, Doctor Lamb. I'll go on back." He disappeared down the hall. "Help you, Munson?"

Ernest excused himself.

Wilber was following Munson upstairs. Overtaking him half way, Ernest said, "I told Lily to tell you not to bother about the early service Sunday. I don't have to preach at eleven, so I'll take it. But if you can get back for Evensong, do."

"I can. I'm going to Paterson to see a lady."

"I know what you're going to Paterson for. And don't get on any strike committee."

"To see a lady, Padre."

"I've told you before not to call me that," Ernest said. "I'm no padre, I'm a priest. You keep that stuff for your Groupers."

"Very good, Your Reverence. May the lady come to supper here?"

"Not unless she comes to the service, too."

"The Test Act," nodded Wilber, grinning. "She's a good girl, Pad—Your Reverence. Now only a healthy pinko. I've snatched her like a brand from the Young Communist League burning. She's got a good head. She's perfectly able to see that atheism isn't an integral part of Communism. It's just a temporary local Russian reaction to a church grown corrupt—"

"Oh, it is, is it? I guess what she's perfectly able to see is your manly charm. But make sure she knows I'm in the pay of the bosses, and it's no good explaining integral parts of Communism, or temporary local Russian reactions, to me. The subjects open to discussion by strangers at my table are art, literature, and Church scandal. Have you got a server for me Sunday morning?"

"Crickey!"

"I ought to make you find one. But never mind. Bill Jennings will do. Go on down and talk to Doctor Lamb for a few minutes. I've just come in and I've got to see who called."

"Something up?"

"A change in the Faiths of Our Neighbors program."

"Not the Rabbi?"

"Who else?"

"Why don't you face the old gent down, sir? I would."

"Yes, I know you would. When you're as worn as I am, you'll stretch forth your hands and another shall gird thee. Get down there and make yourself agreeable. It's a secret,

69

but from what he said, I think he has his diocese lined up, and it won't be Montana, or Olympia, or West Texas. He might be useful to a bright young man who wants to bore from within, so don't tell him what you think of Holy Innocents' endowments."

"Good for him! I hope he gets it. It would be one in the eye for the gaiters on the heights."

"And when you speak of our Bishop, speak of him with respect. Contumacy is a privilege reserved to seasoned Churchmen. I'll be along presently. Take Doctor Lamb into the back room and feed him, if he'll eat."

Wilber had started down. Inspired, he turned now, looked back, glowing with facetious self-satisfaction. "Yea, Lord," he whooped, "thou knowest that I love thee. He saith unto him, Feed my lambs!"

Ernest winced. "Wilber, Wilber," he said.

Groping in his bedroom, Ernest found a light. The windows had been closed and rain lashed over them loudly. Behind the ripple of water down the glass, backyards were lit to broad day in abrupt green incandescence. There was a great toppling crash of thunder.

From under the edge of the ashtray by the telephone Ernest drew Lily's scraps of paper—Bill Jennings, again. Mr. Hawley—*please call Regent*—Lily's tortured numerals could be almost anything. He dropped his hand over the telephone. "She's probably sure she's dying," he thought. A large, sentimental, and infantilely religious woman, Mrs. Hawley would require comfort in the form of convincing detail about the Heaven supposed to be close behind her present miseries. —*With jaspers glow thy bulwarks, Thy streets with emeralds blaze!* If she were really sick, really dying, commonest compassion demanded a promise of these cheap elegances—

The cigarette, tilted smoldering from the side of his

mouth, had a dirty taste. Coughing, almost retching, Ernest pressed it out, annoyed to find, as he did so often, that he had been smoking too much. The ringing of the completed connection drummed at his ear while he rocked, restless, from heel to toe, breathing hard against the smoke-revolted quakes of his stomach. "This is Mr. Cudlipp," he said.

"Who?"

"Mr. Cudlipp. The Vicar of Saint Ambrose's."

"The what?"

"I'm trying to reach Mr. Hawley."

"Mister who?"

"Hawley. Mr. Hawley."

"Never heard of him. You got the wrong number. Good-by."

Ernest broke the connection with his thumb, holding the instrument a moment. He looked vainly about for a telephone directory. Not seeing one, he remained motionless, undecided, for the last time he had noticed Mrs. Hawley—maybe a month ago—he was impressed by her health and vigor. She was, in fact, fond of being ill, as only a person who never really is ill can be.

His eye fell vacantly on the long packed wall of books behind the low bed. Lightning glared behind the windows again. Its thunder seemed to shake the floor under his feet — Ah, there was *The Institutes of the Christian Religion.*

He put down the telephone and pulled the volume out. Fine black dust covered his fingers. He turned a few pages, shook his head, and replaced it. Reading that stuff would be simply impossible for him nowadays—it reflected, if he did, on him; not, certainly, on Calvin. The newest, most urgently readable works of the now popular "Barthian" theology looked, when he let someone like Wilber force him into examining them, just as wearily and long-

71

windedly beside the point. They were all forms of argument. At Wilber's age, it was possible to believe that argument served some purpose, persuaded people, obliged those in error to turn to the truth. But soon enough you would have to wonder if an argument ever did anything beyond giving pleasure to those who already agreed with its contentions. As for those who didn't, they had Moses and the prophets, let them hear them; for you could be sure, after some years with human nature, that though one rose from the dead, far from repenting, they would devote all their energies to evolving a rational explanation for the phenomenon.

But, of course, the warm reception of Barth at the seminary had little to do with the virtue of his theological views. As far as Ernest could judge, the really valuable thing which Doctor Barth did seem to offer was a conception of religious truth which allowed modern-minded young priests like Wilber to recover that sustaining, snobbish ease of mental superiority, loved long since, but, fifty or sixty years ago, lost to the clergy for a while. In these well-cut, stylish new clothes, God could be introduced to any company without embarrassment. Wilber had something for the many scoffers and skeptics he numbered among his liberal and Communist friends.

It was really a walkover. Arguing, as such pagans must, if they were to argue at all, that the Faith was an irrational superstition, they first found themselves standing silly with no opponent. As far as superstition went, Wilber, aided by that other prized import, the German form-criticism, could put the Scriptures through the hoops in a way which made shabby little quibbles, hand-me-downs from Thomas Paine or Colonel Ingersoll, look as infantile as they were.

As for "irrational"—well, were they incapable of understanding that this was essentially a faith of revelation? By its very nature, it was beyond artless attempts to relate it to the categories of a limited reason. This statement was a trap which Wilber sat waiting with relish to snap as soon as any opponent, taking heart from the apparent confession of irrationality, rushed in.

It was hard for an atheist or agnostic to remember that science, once his inexhaustible armory, had been packed up, almost complete, and moved over for Wilber to use. Wilber used it with conscious triumph. So his interlocutor considered religious belief unintelligent, did he? But mightn't that be a snap judgment based on too little study of the evidence? For instance, if he were familiar with the principles and implications of the Riemannian geometry, as they were now being employed, he would certainly understand—in fact, Wilber could run down the line from colloidal chemistry to astrophysics to show that skepticism was out of date, that science had no quarrel with religion. Of course it made not the least impression except on Wilber himself—

The telephone had rung twice, he realized. "Ernest Cudlipp speaking," he said. He raised a new cigarette toward his mouth, but the slight aroma of the unlighted tobacco turned his stomach again. Coughing, he snapped the cigarette to bits between his fingers, tossed the fragments at the wastepaper basket.

"Mr. Cudlipp?"

"Yes, yes."

"Oh, Ernest."

"Yes."

"Carl Willever."

"Carl Will— Why, hello! How are you, Carl?"

"Not very well, in many ways. Do you want to see me?"

"Of course I do. You're in town? Where? At a hotel?"

"I'm at Grand Central."

"Come and stay here. I've plenty of room."

"You hadn't heard I'd left the Order?"

"No," said Ernest, amazed. "I hadn't. Tell me about it."

"The circumstances aren't pleasant. I'll doubtless be leaving the ministry too. And it won't be for 'causes not affecting his moral character.' Do you still want to see me?"

"I don't care what the causes are, Carl. Come over. If I can help you, I will. I'll be delighted to see you."

"You're very kind. I'm afraid I'm rather unpresentable. Father Superior wanted me to take some money; but beyond my ticket, I didn't think I cared to. I was excited and angry. I—"

"Carl, I'm extraordinarily sorry. Come over. Get a night's rest. Tomorrow, tell me as much or as little as you like."

He put down the telephone, perturbed, though he hadn't seen Carl—Father Willever—for five or six years. It must be fully that, and Ernest had to think a moment to remember where.

In Florence. On his way back from a vacation spent— that year he had first heard of them—among the Byzantine remains at Ravenna and Ancona. Father Willever, O.H.T., he found, was to preach at Saint James'. What Father Willever was doing there—surely even the Order of the Holy Trinity wouldn't feel the need to reintroduce catholic practice in Italy—it was impossible to imagine, though afterward easily explained. Carl and the Superior of the Order had been to Lambeth and were making a pilgrimage to Assisi.

At Saint James', a neat, modern, more or less bluntly Protestant version of the local ecclesiastical architecture,

74

Father Willever offered the Holy Sacrifice for the reunion of the Catholic churches. He preached on Devotion to Our Lady, as a topic likely to be of interest to the predominantly feminine congregation. They found it so. Carl Willever was without debate the handsomest man who ever wore his order's white habit. He was ruddy and brown from Franciscan wayfaring (after expressing their luggage, they had come over the mountains from Bologna on foot and planned to proceed to Assisi that way). His voice was sweet, florid, uncomfortably dramatic. Before he had finished, many of the old ladies' eyes were full of tears. Quite a number of the carefully set-apart and chaperoned finishing-school girls were mutely mooning. It was as thick as honey—a revolting saccharine excess, a clear and simple success.

Carl had been in high spirits, charmed to see Ernest. After dinner at the rectory, Carl went with him, or he with Carl, to Fiesole. Carl wanted to walk, but Ernest made him take the tram. They passed the afternoon talking about architecture and what became of men they used to know at the seminary. They had a bad supper with bad wine on a shabby terrace overlooking Florence. Father Willever smoked a cigarette and described the Lambeth Conference. Back again, stepping from a tram under the arc light before the Duomo and the shadowy shape of Giotto's tower, Father Willever clapped him on the shoulder, squeezed his arm. "You're the hardest-shelled P.E. I ever saw, Ernest," he said. "I wish you weren't. I know what to do with the low and lazy. They just never heard of the Catholic Faith. I wish you'd come to Assisi with us. Walk the road Saint Francis walked—"

It was plain that for Carl, too, the afternoon had been a failure.

Ernest said, "Someone's got to stay and minister to the

pew holders. It's really what we're for, you know. Good luck, Carl. Make them put the lights on, so you can see the lower chapel properly."

Remembering this, he stood a moment and remembered back further—other meetings, remarks, gestures. Back to the seminary—Carl had really been a proselyte of Vincent McNamara's. They both had gone to Holy Trinity together; only, six months later, Vincent came out and went right on to Rome, while Carl stayed. The truth was, Carl might not have been a success with the Dominicans. The Order of Preachers wasn't founded in 1890. They knew a vocation when they saw one. Carl simply wasn't the type.

"Ah!" Ernest said, arrested, for on this reflection, Carl, his attitude, his gestures, everything, fell into unmistakable pattern.

"But it couldn't be!" he said. "He couldn't have so little sense—" Yet he knew clearly and coldly that Carl could, Carl had; it was the one possible, perfect explanation.

Obscured by the drive of rain, disappearing altogether in renewed thunder, Ernest heard the piano and Alice singing: "Jesus, lover of my soul, let me to Thy bosom fly. . . ." She was accompanying herself.

It might have been at Mr. Johnston's request, but Ernest guessed suddenly that it wasn't. Alice had volunteered it after Wilber and Doctor Lamb came in, trusting Ernest could hear. Demure, ironic, she would like him to see how suitably she could entertain three strange clergymen. Inspired, she was able to resurrect, doubtless from days when she had been compelled to sing in her father's choir, something which she meant to imply was about their speed.

Ernest laughed. "I'll soon stop that!" he said, rousing himself. He glanced at the last torn paper: *Mr. Wade say not bother.*

76

Lily's slovenly ellipses were familiar to him. No doubt what John had said, finding Ernest out, was for Lily not to bother. He might call again, but he might not, since he had now done his duty and all he wanted to know anyway was whether he considered whatever Ernest had to see him about as important as Ernest did.

"Well," said Ernest, "I'll try to make it important to him! I'll just have to give him his choice—" But John, on the contrary, was the one able to give the choice. Ernest could take him as he was, or turn him out. John was doubtless glad of free lodging, and in his way, fond of Ernest; but only because neither lodging nor Ernest interfered with him. The first time they did—

"And that's the end of that," Ernest said. He threw the crumpled note away. He went downstairs.

Alice had begun the second verse— ". . . hangs my helpless soul on Thee!" Sweet and trusting, her voice went through the motions of hanging up her soul. You could recognize in restrained burlesque the Methodist minister's sanctimonious little daughter showing off to the congregation.

Mr. Johnston had taken it, hook, line, and sinker. The bleak folds and wrinkles of his worn face were softened in ingenuous pleasure. Such a beautiful, inspiring hymn! Such a pretty, reverent woman! Doctor Lamb in the big chair in the corner sat with composed affability. Watching him, you could see the degree to which manners, even among the nominally well-bred, had declined. Doctor Lamb, obliged to remain by the rain, old-fashionedly required himself to find the gathering delightful, the entertainment offered him as a guest excellent. Being bored, or restless, or even politely inattentive, in company would be as much beneath him as appearing there unshaven, in his shirt sleeves.

Munson, poised on the edge of an uncomfortable side

chair beneath a group of three small Syrian ikons, a volume of the scores of some Brahms lieder with difficulty kept closed on his knee, was making such an effort not to fidget that he was fairly sweating. He avoided looking at Alice. Ernest looked then at Wilber, who lounged with extravagant, overjaunty ease beyond the corner of the piano.

Wilber had not been taken in at all. More than that, Ernest saw at once, he was offended. His chubby, agreeable face, not suited to such expressions, was set in comic superciliousness. His brown eyes rested with an irked, sarcastic gleam on Alice. Since she innocently paid no attention to him, he was that much more discomfited. "Cover my defenseless head," she sang, lifting her chin a little as though to let Heaven see how defenseless her red head was, "with the shadow of Thy wing. . . ."

She lowered her eyes meekly, rested her hands a moment, looked over her left shoulder and, thus missing Wilber's disdainful glare, smiled radiantly at Ernest. "Shall I go on, Ernie?" she asked.

"By no means!" said Ernest. "That will be more than enough. Let Mr. Munson take the piano. Perhaps Doctor Lamb would prefer Brahms."

"Oh, Vicar," protested Wilber. He indicated the irony impending by letting his voice rise to a falsetto. "We were so hoping Mrs. Breen would sing 'Rock of Ages' next."

The retort was better than Ernest would have expected from Wilber—except for its, alas, inept delivery. That was marked enough to make even Doctor Lamb regard Wilber with surprise.

Ernest said, "You can sing it to yourself while you are going downstairs to get the rector a cold bottle of beer. You'd like some, wouldn't you, Doctor?"

"Thank you," said Doctor Lamb, imperturbably dismissing the whole incident, "I would enjoy one." To Alice he said, facing her with frank approval—in his dispassionate way there was nothing Doctor Lamb liked better than a pretty, smartly dressed woman—"That was delightful, Mrs. Breen. I think Mr. Cudlipp is too hard on the simple old hymns. I always like to hear them."

Almost pouting, Wilber had gone out. Ernest turned and called, "Just a moment." Wilber was waiting at the stair head, still sulky. "Ask Lily to see what she can do about making some sandwiches." Ernest smiled, shaking his head a little. "And don't be rude, Wilber. It's all right to run around with your revolutionary friends, but don't let yourself start acting like them. You haven't any need to. For various good reasons, they all have inferiority complexes, and so they can't be teased without getting huffy. None of us liked that last remark of yours. Now, make an effort."

Wilber swallowed, tightened his lips in the required effort. "Okay, Padre," he said. His natural amiability triumphed. He smiled, laughed briefly. "Sorry. Well, as a matter of fact, it *is* an inferiority complex. A psychological disability."

He got the uncomfortable moment of reproof behind him by joining impartially in the criticism of himself. "I ought to be able to rationalize it, of course. But it's hard. I don't mind having a man imply that I'm a simpleton or a sissy, or I wouldn't be in the Church. But I'm not so good at taking it from a woman. I think it's because we don't feel sure where we stand. One of the fellows over at Sem. —graduate student, and really a brilliant chap, even if he is too spike for comfort—name's Clarke. I want to have him meet you sometime—was discussing the whole matter of celibacy of the clergy in my rooms the other night—"

Ernest could almost have loved Wilber for a simplicity so fresh and charming. But, ah, those intricate, endless

79

seminary discussions! Those knowing graduate students, so brilliant, daring, paradoxical! Those urgent, dramatic spikes with a *Missale Romanum* in their back pockets and a complete scheme to save the Papacy's face and still get around the *Apostolicae Curae!* Those aloof, pallid, chronically constipated mystics with their Deeper Insight! Those robust, cold-bath-taking young men who knew Jesus personally—used to go to school with Him, in fact! "I hate to think of it," Ernest said sincerely.

"Oh, I don't by any means hold with him in his conclusions," Wilber said. "But if celibacy were part of our discipline, it is true that we'd know where we stood. And so would the women. It would be all settled."

Ernest said, "You'll find it settled in the Thirty-second Article. Completely settled. And I would strongly advise the Dean to suppress such discussions. Now, be good enough to get the—"

"Ah, in that sense!" Wilber said. He grasped the stair rail. "Yes. Granted. But in the practical, the practicable, sense, nothing is settled. Not by a long shot! You might as well say that the Twenty-eighth Article settles our attitude toward the Real Presence. It simply hedges. It lets you believe what you like—"

"And what more could anyone ask?" said Ernest. "Now get downstairs—"

"No, but honestly, sir. That's the whole difficulty. Paul pretty well expressed—"

"Saint Paul, Saint Paul, if you mean the apostle. You aren't a Unitarian. And I already know the things he well expressed."

"Well, the point is, you feel as if you were neither bond nor free. You can go courting, if you like; but you have to go in a rabat, so to say. And you have to be pretty thick skinned if that doesn't fuss you any. Sure, marriage signifies to us the mystical union that is betwixt Christ and the Church. But if all you want to do is signify a mystical union, you haven't any business asking a normal young woman to marry you. If what you want is to get her into bed—well, as Clarke says, look at it anyway you like, it's neither spiritual, edifying, nor indicative of a whole mind in God's work for the Reverend Mr. N. or M. to signify a mystical union betwixt his consecrated office and his hot pants—"

"I had my doubts about this Clarke," Ernest said. "I now have more of them. In my day, there used always to be a few fellows who sat around like that making matriculants blush; but in this enlightened age how can it be worth the effort? Anyway, your Groupers have solved all those problems for you, haven't they? Now, for the last time, get down there!"

"Well, what I meant to say was"—Wilber persisted, starting down—"that it makes for a very real complex in most cases. I haven't escaped it. I know it—"

"And now you've told me. And I think it's all right. There's no real reason to be embarrassed because your clerical collar keeps you from feeling free to proposition every woman you meet. Many of them don't even expect it, so you can be just as celibate as you want."

From the bottom of the stairs Wilber said, "Okay, Padre. That's what I'll be."

Wilber was restored. Having done his best to make an important thought clear to Ernest, he now gave up tolerantly. The Vicar was set in his preconceptions and prejudices. You had to expect it and make allowances. As one got older, one lost the capacity to see things as they were, and saw them, instead, distorted by habit and familiarity. There was nothing to be done about it.

Wilber went whistling toward the kitchen, where he

could be heard greeting Lily. Lily made some doleful response, and he cried heartily, "Why, Lily, don't tell me a sensible woman like you is afraid of thunder! Of course you're not!"

But of course Lily was. She, too, was set in her preconceptions and prejudices. Wilber was cheery, patient, and sympathetic with her; for she was a funny, good-hearted old girl, and couldn't, after all, help her natural obtuseness.

Munson played the piano. The music was not familiar to Ernest, but apparently it was to Alice, for she sang with ease and alacrity in fairly good German. About to go in, he thought he heard the outer door open, and he turned quickly. If it was Carl Willever, so soon, the only thing to do would be to take him upstairs. Doctor Lamb was almost sure to know him. Father Willever's reputation as a preacher and as a prominent figure in the High Church party was great enough to make his point of view useful to those who were anxious for harmony or unity in the Church. Doctor Lamb could hardly help having met him, or corresponded with him.

Under the circumstances, it wouldn't be desirable to have them meet again. Ernest waited a moment while Wilber came, whistling still, up from the basement with several bottles. He went on, not seeing Ernest, into the back room. There had been no knock or ring, so the front door might merely have blown open. Ernest closed his hand on the handle of the vestibule door. He faced, with disconcerting abruptness, Lulu Merrick. Motionless, her eyes closed, she leaned against the strip of vestibule wall.

"Lu!" he said, shocked. "You're soaked! What on earth have you been doing?"

She opened her eyes and looked at him, but made no response. He said: "Go upstairs at once and take that dress off. Lily will bring you a bathrobe. We'll try to get that dried. Come."

She continued to stare, stupid and stupefied. The cheap printed cloth stuck to her sagging shoulders, clung damply to her ungainly thighs and knees. She wore no hat. The hard rain had plastered her thinning hair to her head— draggled wisps of it, the blonde gone off, grown wholly gray, dank now with water, hung on her forehead. "Come," he repeated. He took her by the forearm, feeling the flesh, clammy, grossly spongy under his fingers. He started upstairs with her.

At perhaps the sixth step, she slumped definitely against him, her foot failing to reach the next rise. "Lu!" he said. He caught the rail in one hand, bracing himself with difficulty. "Have you had anything to eat today?"

"I had some coffee this morning," she said faintly.

"Why didn't you eat something?"

"I didn't have the money."

"Where have you been all day?"

"I sat in the ferry house. I telephoned you. And then I started to walk up here. I didn't have any money."

"Good God!" said Ernest. "Now, hold onto the rail." Still supporting her, he called, "Wilber! I want you a moment."

"Coming, sir."

"Quick. Lend me a hand. Mrs. Merrick isn't feeling well. We'll put her in John Wade's room and she can lie down."

Wilber bounded around the newel post and, two steps at a time, upstairs. "All right, sir," he said. "I've got her. I think I'd better pick her right up."

His face swelled with the effort, but he did it. He began laboriously to climb. Ernest snapped on the light in the

83

hall. He swung open the door of John's room. "Just lay her on the cot," he said. "And would you run down and tell Lily to come up here at once— Lu," he said, shaking her shoulder. "I don't like her looks at all. Ask Mr. Johnston to come up too. He knows something about medicine." He put on another light.

Lulu said, not opening her eyes, "I'm all right, Ernie. Just let me lie down a minute."

Her color was already a little better, and he called, "Wilber, never mind about Mr. Johnston, for the moment. Tell Lily; and there's some aromatic spirits in one of the bathrooms. See if you can find it." He sat on the edge of the cot. "Lu," he said, "why do you do it?"

"Do what?"

"Come to town this way. This is the fourth time since April. You must stay at Belvidere. There, you have your board, and a roof over your head. Now, what are you going to do for money to get back? You'll have to take it from either me or Edna. Can't you see that it's not fair? Neither of us is well off. It's all we can do to find the money for Mrs. Blair. I haven't, at this moment, five dollars in my pocket. I'll have to borrow some for you. It isn't like you to do this sort of thing. Now, what's the trouble? Why did you come?"

She said falteringly, "I can't stay at Mrs. Blair's any longer, Ernie. I can't stay at Belvidere. I can't stand that awful little town—" Her voice gained energy, half fear, half anger, like a child yelling, "No! No! No!," with the double purpose of drowning out objections and distracting his own mind by hearty noise from the punishment he was surely inviting. "New Jersey's so terrible!" she said. "I think I'll go to Woodstock, or Provincetown. I might be able to start a tea room, or something—"

To answer Lulu it was necessary to deny that life in Belvidere was impossible. That would be intricate and exhausting. For a moment Ernest was tempted to make no denial. After all, when they brought Lulu down there, he had seen Mrs. Blair's boarding house. He could see still the vile faded wall-papers, the worn hangings which made each gloomy room gloomier. From the smell of cooking, mingled with the musty smell of the old house, it was easy to form an idea of the food scorched in cheap greases, or boiled to a pale slop. Glimpses of Belvidere showed a small, mean, dirty town disfigured by its manufactures. What was new—an eruption of bungalows around it—bad and ugly. What was old—one or two eighteenth-century houses standing shaky and neglected, breaks in the dreary business blocks—guaranteed a decay from which no one now living could hope to see any recovery. As for the state of New Jersey—

But, of course, that wasn't Lulu's trouble. Her spirits weren't the delicate, overpampered sort which could be sunk by sad or squalid surroundings. The phrases of her complaint, apparently so apt, so true, so pointed (how could you send her back there? *Whatsoever ye would that men should do to you*—) were not to be taken literally. What she meant by the awfulness of Belvidere, the impossibility of Mrs. Blair's, the terrors of New Jersey, came out in the mention of the tea room.

Lulu yearned vainly back to her miraculous years. Since they had begun when she started the Button Box, and ended when the Button Box finally failed, she would go to her grave believing that everything must, in the same inexplicable way as before, be all right if she could only start another place. She was simply incapable of seeing that the Button Box failed because it was finished, because she was finished. It lived its eight or nine years not on good management or good food, or on any capability or aptitude of Lulu's which she might still have and might again exploit.

To begin with, people went there because everyone had been shocked by the death of a painter so young, so well liked; it was then thought, so brilliant, as Ronald Merrick. They resolved, in a passion of generous sentiment, to do something for Ronald's beautiful young wife and child. Once begun, the business continued, even prospered markedly, through its convenience; and then, as a habit, so long as enough people who remembered Ronald and knew Lulu remained in the neighborhood. Its end was thus embodied in its beginning, its failure in its first success. In the end, they all had departed, disappeared.

Ernest ate there regularly. It was just a few doors from the artily made-over flats, belonging to Saint Matthew's, where he lived. Sometimes, in some moods, it was possible to remember the talk, the people, the atmosphere, with pleasure; but, more and more, when the Button Box came to mind, Ernest was only dismayed by the uncountable hours, his own and a hundred other people's, passed profitlessly over those bare board tables. Seen this way, the Button Box was a not implausible form for hell—a subterranean great room crowded by tables all crowded with people, all talking at once. The close, smoke-veiled air rang with their boasts and pretenses, their fatuous hopes, their spites and vanities and elaborate emotions; while they waited for food, while they ate it, while they waited afterward to see who might come in. As in hell, no doubt, the average patron could look forward to seeing everyone he ever knew come in sooner or later.

Of course Ronald was soon forgotten. His paintings, which hung on the walls, no longer seemed particularly brilliant. Even the famous nude called *Breathing Spell*, cause of a tremendous uproar when an officer of the Society for the Suppression of Vice brought it into court because of its realistic detail, seemed to lose some of its daring when it became no longer obvious, or even credible, that Lulu had been the model.

But for a time Lulu survived on her past. Probably she more than survived, she flourished still in many memories as beautiful, eloquent, wonderfully intelligent, marvelously witty. In fact, she had never been anything but easily pleased, and so happy; and being happy, agreeable to have around. Soon she had begun to lose her looks. In five years she had lost them entirely. They must have depended on a perishable blondeness which bound them mysteriously together; made her skin and hair seem ravishing, her figure and movement full of grace; even gave her the appearance of quick, candid intelligence. With youth gone, they were gone, too. And then, you might think, with them gone, in gradual progressive ruin, everything went, for her looks had been all there was to her. Until, today—

"That's not possible at the moment," Ernest said. "You can't start it on nothing. And no one will finance you, Lu. Not at present. Not until you show that you can be trusted, that you will work, and that you won't drink. It's up to you."

Ernest could hear his voice, glib in the habit of admonition. Practice made his manner and tone ring professionally true, not to be questioned. In part he could excuse his insincerity by his kindness. How cruel and useless to face facts, to be honest with Lulu, to let her see that things were not merely as bad as in her dejection she thought, but far worse—worse than she had the intelligence or perception to realize unassisted. Yet, of course, he spoke, too, to spare Ernest, to delude her into hoping, no matter for what, so long as it got her quietly off his hands and away to a place where she could realize her despair without bothering him—

"Lu," he said, "Edna and I can't do more than we're do-

87

ing. You must go back to Belvidere and be patient. Lie down, and I'll have some food brought. I can't keep you here. I'll telephone Edna and she can put you up. In the morning she'll see you get a train back."

She answered nothing.

He could hear Lily plodding and groaning on the stairs. At the top she panted, "You want me, Mr. Cudlipp?"

"In there, Lily," said Wilber.

"I can find him," she answered tartly.

Ernest came into the hall. "Help Mrs. Merrick get that dress off, take it down and dry it as well as you can. Bring up something to eat. Make her some tea."

"How'm I to dry a thing without fire?" asked Lily. "We got not a crumb to eat."

"Make a fire. Find something." He went into his bedroom, dropped on the divan, swung his legs up and lay wearily on his back, the telephone resting across his cheek. "Edna," he said.

"Hello, Ernie. How are you?"

"Worn out, my dear. Lulu's in town."

"Oh, my God!"

"Yes. I'll have to send her down."

"Oh, my God."

"I heard you the first time. I think she'll go back. She got restless. I'll have to write Mrs. Blair. She must have cooked up some story and got the money from her."

"Unless she stole it. Is she drunk?"

"No."

"Ernie, I'm pretty sick of this. Aren't you?"

"Yes. But let's get her back. Then we'll have to think about it."

"All right, Ernie. Don't take it to heart so. I've a damned good mind to give her enough veronal to fix her."

"Don't say the word," Ernest said. "I've had one bout with women and veronal this evening, as it happens. Good night, my dear. I'll get her down in about an hour—with some money for her ticket."

"If you give her a cent, you're insane."

"I'll send someone with her."

He put the telephone on the stand, looking at the light glowing orange through his closed eyelids. The storm was passing. Most of the thunder had moved far on to the east, but he could hear the rain. In the room below the piano continued.

Wilber said, standing in the door, "Anything wrong, sir?"

Ernest blinked, opening his eyes. "Yes," he said, sitting up. "Myself when young. There is no known remedy."

"You might try a couple of aspirin tablets," Wilber said, "or a good night's sleep."

"Don't you patronize me, you puppy," Ernest snorted. "I'll do the patronizing around here." He got to his feet. "Come. Let's see if the rector isn't ready to be eased out. We'll get him a taxi."

"It's quicker to pick one up," Ernest said. "Some of the big companies have garages over there. They come through in droves. Wilber can just stand in the door and wave one over."

"I'm sorry to leave," Doctor Lamb said. "It has been most enjoyable. Most enjoyable. Thank you so much, Mrs. Breen. Thank you, Mr. Munson."

He turned and shook hands with Mr. Johnston. "I have a favor to ask of you. I promised the Women's Auxiliary that I'd see if I couldn't persuade you to talk to them sometime during the fall about the Church's work in the North. They were all most interested. If you'd care to do it, we could arrange it at your convenience. Meetings are on second Thursdays at eleven."

Taken by surprise, Mr. Johnston nodded, confused;

looking aside toward Ernest. "That's an excellent plan, Doctor," Ernest said. "Mr. Johnston has had remarkable experiences. It would do any Women's Auxiliary good to hear them."

"Splendid!" said Doctor Lamb. "I'll have Miss Stoddard get their schedule to you, and we can work out a date. Good night, Mrs. Breen. Thank you again. Good night, Mr. Munson."

In the hall he said, "I hope I didn't intrude." He added quietly, "Mr. Johnston. Is he well, Cudlipp? Is too much being asked of him? I wonder if it was wise to put him where the work is so strenuous? Well, you must let me know."

"I think he enjoys it," Ernest said. "He seems anxious to do all he can."

"Yes. But we must face the fact that there are two sides to it. If it proves that you and Mr. Quinn are doing your work and his, too—we can't have that. We all know from experience that it can't be handled that way."

The doors were open and Wilber stood in them against the flood of street light and the slow, failing descent of raindrops. "There we are, sir," he called. "Got one."

"Good. Good. Thank you, Quinn. I've meant to tell you I thought that was a most interesting letter of yours in the *Churchman* a week or so ago. You had a nice point. . . ."

Now they stood in the vestibule. The cab came slanting to the curb below and halted. The driver's left hand swung back to the door handle, his right knocked up the meter flag.

"Oh," said Doctor Lamb, "I believe that's engaged—"

A man in a worn gray felt hat and a shabby brown suit stepped, bent, into the rain; straightened up, said something to the driver. As he started toward the sandstone steps, he saw the three of them in the door and called,

"Oh, Ernest! Lend me a dollar to pay this fellow, will you? I haven't any change—"

Ernest stepped in front of Doctor Lamb, went quickly down. "Carl," he said. "Go in. Go in. There are some people in the back room. I'm on the second floor, in back, right above it."

He paid the man without haste. "Wait," he said, "here's another fare for you."

Glancing up, he saw Carl Willever reach the door. Wilber and Doctor Lamb drew back to let him in. Doctor Lamb gave him a keen, attentive glance. "All right, sir," Ernest called.

Doctor Lamb shook hands hastily with Wilber, came down through the light rain. It hadn't worked, Ernest saw. He said, "That was Carl Willever."

"You don't mean—" said Doctor Lamb. "But, of course! That's who I thought it was! I seldom forget a face. What on earth—"

"I don't know. He telephoned me this evening. He said he'd left the Order."

"Dear me," said Doctor Lamb, standing still, the rain forgotten. "I don't like to hear that. What a sad thing for them at Holy Trinity, after all these years. Is he going over to Rome? I suppose so. What a pity they can't see their way clear from the start. Think of the doubt and distress he's going to cause hundreds of devout people! I can't help wondering if a man in his prominent position is really free to— There, we're both getting wet! Tell him I'm sorry not to have spoken to him. I didn't recognize him until too late. Go on. Good night, my dear fellow."

Wilber, waiting in the hall, closed the door after Ernest. "I'll run along, sir," he said. "Did you hear that about the *Churchman*?" He rocked with laughter. "Do you know what the letter was about?"

"No," said Ernest, more brusquely than he intended. "But you gave me a copy and I'll find out sometime." He smiled. "Sorry, Wilber. You're very patient with me. I don't know why everything happens at once, unless it's for my sins. Lord, what an evening!"

"It looks about as usual to me," Wilber said. "Don't ask me how you stand it. I think you ought to take a vacation, sir."

"No doubt. Did you hear that that Jennings brat is in jail? I can't decide what to do about it. They picked him up by a particularly raw trick; but I'm prepared to believe they had their reasons. I don't like to take the matter to Judge Noseda, because I don't think the boy's worth it. Noseda's done me a number of favors in handling cases I've mentioned to him. Naturally he gets tired of it. What do you think?"

"I think Jimmy's a bad egg," Wilber said. "But he's never had a chance. The only miracle is that Bill isn't just like him. You know what I think about that, Padre. He's the natural product of a society in which property is the source of privilege—until we change that, we won't get anywhere."

"Until we get somewhere, how will we change that?" asked Ernest, exasperated. "Your friends downtown aren't getting anywhere, Wilber. They're sentimentalists. They don't believe in the doctrine of original sin. Realists are the only people who get things done. A realist does the best he can with things as they are. Don't waste your time trying to change things so you can do something. Do something, do your Christian duty, and in time you may hope things will change"—he put a cigarette in his mouth—"or, rather, do exactly as you wish, but please don't argue. I didn't mean to start it. Since you're going downtown, I wish you'd take Mrs. Merrick with you, and drop her at an address I'll give you. Have you any money?"

"Only about ten dollars, I'm afraid."

"I seem to have three. Here are two of them for the taxi. I've telephoned Edna—it's Mrs. Stone—and you deliver Mrs. Merrick to her in person—regardless of how plausible Mrs. Merrick is about any other plan. If you can spare five dollars, give it to Mrs. Stone for Mrs. Merrick's ticket. I'll pay you Sunday."

"Right. Don't you worry, sir. I'll get her there."

Gently but firmly, Wilber would. You could rely on him, not merely in great matters of principle, but in every small matter. When he failed, it was only poor judgment, or human forgetfulness. As far as his intention enabled him to be, he was perfect in the first-named fruit of the spirit. What more could you ask of any man? You could ask better sense!

Ernest went to the door of the back room and looked in. All the lights had been turned out but the one by the piano. Beyond the three battered ikons gleaming on the wall, Alice lay back in the shadow, a cigarette between her fingers, her eyes half closed. In his chair, Mr. Johnston was relaxed too. His arms lay sagging on his knees. His head hung. He was asleep.

At the piano, Munson, absorbed face lifting and falling as his shoulders moved to the swift easy movement of his flexible hands, was playing softly—the G-major Nocturne, Ernest realized, surprised.

Munson never played Chopin. At least, Ernest never heard him playing any; but of course he couldn't play it like that unless it was perfectly familiar to him. Very likely, Ernest thought, touched by the simplicity of the idea, all the Chopin Munson knew had painful emotional or sentimental associations for him. He did not often feel like playing it.

Alice's eyes moved a little, and Ernest lifted a hand,

spoke the words *one moment,* soundlessly. She brought her own hand up and blew him a kiss.

Upstairs he stood outside John's room and called, "Lu, Mr. Quinn is going to take you down to Edna's. Are you ready?"

Lily said, "She'll be ready in a minute, Mr. Cudlipp."

"And, Lily," he added, "there'll be five breakfasts in the morning. I'm putting a friend in the room upstairs by Mr. Munson." He turned back and entered his bedroom.

Carl Willever sat on the divan, turning the pages of the German quarto. He snapped it shut and threw it aside. He said, "This suit, as you can see, isn't mine. It belongs to Brother Robert, a little enthusiast who's never, never, never going to have any further use for it. What a damned fine touch your pianist downstairs has. It's a long while since I've heard any Chopin."

He did look at Ernest. "Well, I think I'll be going," he said roughly. "I saw your rector giving me the eye. I never did like that man, and I know he never liked me; though we often exchanged compliments in print and elsewhere for diplomatic reasons. You couldn't lend me— No; to hell with that fancy stuff! You couldn't give me a couple of dollars, could you?"

"I literally couldn't, tonight," Ernest said. "But I can give you a bed, which you need more; and we'll talk about it tomorrow. Now, let's call it a day."

"If you want to talk, we might as well talk now, and get it over. I don't know why I called you up. Yes, I do. I didn't know anyone else to call, and I didn't know how I was going to eat, tomorrow. Well, plenty of people don't eat. I guess I can learn. If you can't give me a couple of dollars, could you give me a quarter?"

"Come upstairs, and I'll show you where you sleep. You'll have to sleep somewhere. You're dead on your feet now. I don't want to hear about it tonight. It's too late."

Carl Willever stood up. "Sure," he said, "I'll get out. You always were the smuggest bastard, Ernest. You always knew best. Even in the seminary you were a knowing little shrimp sitting around with that pop-eyed supercilious look while other men were doing the best they could to work out a way of life. You had us all fooled. You can't tell me you believe any of this nonsense—all the little angels ass-end up! You just get a kick out of seeing the boobs take what you give them—"

"Come on, come on," said Ernest. "Go to bed, Carl. Here are some pajamas."

"That's right. Him that taketh away thy cloak, forbid not to take thy coat also! You think I don't know you sniveling Christians by this time? You feel pretty good, don't you—just like Jesus, God damn you—" Gulping and groaning, he began to sob.

"Shut up!" snapped Ernest. "The house is full of people. Now, be quiet and get upstairs. I won't have it."

The tears crowded shining out of Carl Willever's swollen eyes. His face crumpled, disfigured. "Go to hell!" he cried. "Let go of me—"

Ernest was bringing him into the hall. Still holding Carl's arm, he doubled his fist, drove it as hard as he could into Carl's ribs. "Stop that!" he said. "Do you think I'm joking?"

They went around the corner of the stair rail, Carl making no further resistance, and started for the third floor. The door of John's room opened and Lulu came out. Her face swung dumbly up toward them. "Now, you just go along," said Lily. "I need my rest. I toil the whole day, from crack of dawn—"

"That will do, Lily," Ernest said. "Go on down, Lu. I'll be there." To Carl he said, "That room. The light's by the

95

door. You'll find bedding on the bed. That's the bath-room, there." Not inviting, or waiting for, any response, he turned down the long stairs again.

Wilber had seen Lily and Lulu coming. He went out to stop another taxi. Lulu sat down on the chair in the hall. Lily started for the back stairs to the basement. Hearing Ernest, she stopped, gave him a reproachful look. It was easy to see that Lulu didn't please her. Her voice sank to an indistinct mumble, but a person used to hearing her could understand her to remark, put-upon and disapprov-ing, "That trash wearies me."

"Yes," said Ernest, "and I want no more impertinence from you. Have coffee up at eight."

Lily disappeared slowly downstairs, accompanied by re-newed, still less distinct mumbling, which would be a justification of her attitude, with some mention of her pa-tience and virtue.

Lulu said: "Ernie—"

He turned to her, resigned to a protest about this dis-posal of her, but she continued uncertainly: "Who's that awful crying man up there? What's he there for—"

"He's in trouble," Ernest said.

She answered, "Oh," vaguely.

Her change of tone startled Ernest. The aimless lapse from consternation to apathy was so marked that he found himself for the first time thinking of one other possible so-lution to the problem of her future. After all, she was Stel-la's mother. Liquor, if she were managing to get hold of it often; or, even, mere unbearable anxiety and discourage-ment might very well send her the way syphilis and co-deine had so quickly taken Stella.

Wilber said: "We're all ready, Mrs. Merrick."

Ernest took her hand between his. "Good-by, Lu," he said. "Write me when you get back. Edna and I will do all

96

we can. You mustn't worry. You must be patient. We love you. Remember that, won't you?" He kissed her cheek.

Wilber led her down the steps. From the bottom, he called, "Good night, sir."

In the back room Munson had stopped playing. Mr. Johnston was awake again. He was struggling stiffly to his feet as Ernest came in. He put his glasses on. To Alice and Munson he said in great embarrassment, "I'm afraid I dozed off a moment! I beg your pardon—well, that's a sign I should be in bed."

"So should we all," Ernest said. They came into the hall. Alice had probably just finished telling Munson how wonderful he was. Munson was still warm and red, his eyes shining with pleasure and the excitement of his music. She put out a hand and he took it diffidently. Turning, she offered it to Mr. Johnston. "Good night," she said. "I hope we'll meet again." Her practiced smile passed sweet and warm over him. In confusion, he stammered, "Yes, indeed. Yes, indeed."

"Good night, Mrs. Breen," said Munson. They started upstairs.

"I'm going to Harriet's," she told Ernest. "I said I would when I called. I'll stay, in the morning, and see your young woman through, if you like—supposing Harriet thinks it's all right. Of course she won't do it if—"

"Of course she won't," said Ernest firmly, lifting his eyebrows. "Where is this Harriet? I'll take you there."

"Oh, oh," said Alice. "Sorry."

She glanced up toward Munson and Mr. Johnston. "Méfiez-vous," she whispered, "les oreilles ennemies vous écoutent! Do you remember those signs? Oh, dear, I'm getting old, Ernie. Wasn't the war wonderful! I know it isn't the thing to say so, nowadays; but do you remember Paris in nineteen-eighteen?"

97

"I ought to," Ernest said. "I'd forgotten you were there."

"I met you once or twice."

"What were you doing?"

"Wearing one of those frightful cross red suits, and losing my virtue.'

"None of it struck me as very gay."

"Maybe not, sub specie aeternitatis—isn't that right? I got it from Lee's monk. But all the world was young, and everybody had something pretty important and exciting to do, and the lid was off, because it was going to go on forever, and there was no use making plans or being sensible—"

"And you still think that's a wonderful state?"

"Don't be so commendable, Ernie! I'll bet that nine of every ten people who reached France and didn't get blown up personally had the time of their lives. No wonder we're arranging for another."

"No wonder," said Ernest.

"All right. I'm sorry I said it. I think I'll walk to Harriet's. It's only a few blocks over. And you don't have to come."

"Come on," he said.

The air was fresh in the street. Pavements were still shining wet. They walked west in silence to the corner. The gutter was full of wide shallow water and Alice made a face, caught up the folds of her skirt, and jumped it nimbly. "You'll ruin your shoes," he said.

"Why not?" she asked. "Tomorrow Lee's going to have to buy me a lot more than new shoes."

He took her arm, steadying her, and they passed under the pillars of the elevated. "What's been happening all evening?" she asked. "Doctor Lamb and I were consumed with curiosity."

"Lulu was here. I sent her down to Edna Stone's."

"What's wrong with her?"

"Many things."

"Why don't you want to tell me?"

"Because it's a stupid, tedious story. I don't dwell on it. And what can I tell you? She has lost her looks. She has lost her friends. She has lost her money. Not improbably, she is losing her mind."

"Ernie."

"Yes, my dear?"

"I'd like to ask you something. Probably you won't tell me."

"Probably I won't, if I think there's no reason to."

"I've wondered, off and on, for years. Was there ever anything between you and her?"

"Was there ever anything between you and that little Polish wench—whatever her name was—who acted too?"

"How horrible of you to remember that!" said Alice. "No. I mean, not in any real emotional sense. Yes, if you mean—"

"I don't want to know the details," said Ernest. "Chasten yourself with them."

"Oh, I do. Though I wouldn't mind at all, if there had been any real feeling. It's when you've been dishonest with yourself that you hate to—"

"Bunk," said Ernest. "Do you think a sin is less a sin, or a stupidity less stupid, because you sincerely want to commit it? Resist this horrid nonsense about being true to yourself. All you mean by it is that, regardless of intelligence or integrity, you are resolved to gratify every random impulse. It's conduct unbecoming a rational being."

"What I mean by it is that I try not to let fear or vanity make my decisions for me. I think it's admirable of me to feel that way. You didn't answer my question."

"I don't purpose to."

"Well, then you see what I have to think."

"It is what you must have thought anyway. You should be very suspicious of what appears to be evidence to support you in a preconception."

"God, how learned!"

"You aren't just walking for the exercise, are you?" asked Ernest. "Because I don't need any."

"No, darling. It's one more over, and one up. I think your Wilber is very cute. How he hates me! Did he think I was making fun of him? Your Mr. Johnston is certainly a lamb. And so is Doctor Lamb, except he looks a good deal more like a tough old ewe. You're really all marvelous." She giggled. "You know, Lee's going to think I spent the night with you."

"Now, you're getting silly," said Ernest. "And Lee isn't going to think any such thing."

"I know it," she yawned. "God, I'm so tired, I could die. Did your little poet come home? I hoped you'd introduce him to me. I could lead him astray properly, I'll bet. What a load off your mind."

"Stop it, Alice," he said. "We're going to have a serious quarrel in a moment."

"Oh, darling, darling! I'm sorry. Here we are. Tell your girl to come over about ten and ask for me. I'll take her down to the office—" She rested a hand on his shoulder, kissed the side of his chin. "Good night. I'll call you."

"Good night, my dear," he said.

———— • ————

Stretched on the low couch in the dark, his hands locked behind his head, Ernest closed his eyes against the faint radiance, the dark reflection of the cloudy sky, luminous with the city lights. There was still an occasional drip of water from the long past rain.

Ernest breathed steadily, sleepless, turning over unwillingly the hard, hot day; but he was tired beyond interest or conclusion. He thought of Carl Willever upstairs—how strange he would find it, for a long while to come, to be sleeping not in his narrow cell, not under the plain crucifix. He thought of John, probably good and drunk and behaving like an egregious jackass somewhere. He thought of Geraldine stretched out drugged in the expensive, almost unfurnished apartment, and reached for the small pad and silver pencil in the drawer of the stand. Supporting the pad against his palm, he started to write in the dark: *Call Mrs.*— His mind, blank, surprisingly refused her married name and he laid the pencil down.

"Ah, ah!" he thought, wincing, "the wren goes to't and the small gilded fly—" Lulu's sad, alcoholic face oppressed him—the shapeless waist, the prolapsed belly sagging in the cheap cloth. He thought of Alice's light carrot-colored hair, the fine, powdered, delicately freckled skin; her hands laid on the piano keys, her breasts bound toward each other by some undergarment. "Not above what ye are able!" he thought.

His weariness was as acute as physical pain. He lifted his stinging eyelids on the imperfect darkness of the room, made out the wooden Saint Ambrose silent in obscurity; hacked narrow feet clutching the beehive, the broken scroll proffered by the mutilated hand. "Like the saints," he said aloud, "thought purges me, labor purifies me, the Old Man rightly disgusts me!"

In the Italian river, they stood to their shanks, Saint Ambrose cupping up water. His worn palm dashed it on Saint Augustine's head. They stared at each other in a passionate, fanatical surmise, until, without premeditation their mouths fell open, chanting the spontaneous antiphon: *We praise thee, O God; we acknowledge thee to be the Lord . . .*

Leadenly, snoring, Ernest slept.

TWO

ORNING SUN blazed across
the backs of all the houses on this side of the block. The
air was soft. It was so mild that it seemed to have no tem-
perature at all. Windless, it was full of a golden haze and
the enormous general stir of the city.

"Wait a minute!" called Ernest. "I haven't any clothes
on." He kicked off the sheet twisted about him, found an
old silk dressing gown on the floor. "Come," he said,
"come!"

The door bumped open with a rattle of crockery.
"Morning, Mr. Cudlipp," Lily said sourly. She made a
space on the bedside table to set down the round tray on
which were jumbled a small teapot full of coffee, a
chipped cup too big for its saucer, and a plate with some
honey and several crescent rolls in a napkin.

"I bring up the five trays you tell me," she resumed,
"but Mr. Wade never sleep in his bed. He's not there."

"Then he won't want any breakfast," Ernest said.

From under her arm Lily produced a morning paper
and a mass of mail. "Here," she said. Outside, she groaned

102

loudly as she stooped to pick up John's tray, which she must have put on the floor. Muttering, she dragged herself downstairs.

Ernest went into the bathroom. From the one directly above sounded the fast muffled crash of a shower, and Munson whistling "La donna è mobile." Ernest nodded, pleased to know that Munson had been able to keep overnight the satisfactions of his successful evening; and amused, too; for it was agreeable to visualize Munson, his solemn face longer and solemner than ever, as he stood in the spray, pursed his lips, and trilled soberly measures so rollicking and trivial.

Returning to his bedroom, Ernest threw the cushions back on the divan, settled against them, and poured himself coffee. As was usually the case, it had cooled a good deal. He swallowed it in three gulps, smeared a crescent roll with honey and stuffed it in his mouth while he sorted out the envelopes on the bed.

A half a dozen of them were bills, to remind him that he was really up against it about money. "Lord," he said, "I must pay Frazer for those books; and I must not order any more. At least, I must pay him something on account. I've got to manage that. He needs the cash—"

Ernest threw the bills aside, leafed over the remaining letters—the one with Spanish stamps would be Oliver Brown. He almost opened it; but the next was turned backward and on the flap he saw embossed the Order of the Holy Trinity's black trefoil of looped cord. He lit a cigarette and tore the end from the envelope: *Dear Fr. Cudlipp: I understand that Carl Willever, who has recently left us, is expecting to see you. I pray that you may be of help to him. The great pain and grief we feel moves me to let you know, for his information, that we all are, and will always be, ready to receive him back in charity and comradeship. I do not want him to imagine that any action or attitude of ours puts added difficulty in the way of his repentance and restoration. I hope you will see fit to mention this letter to him—Yours faithfully in Christ—*

Without, himself, feeling any special sympathy for the High Church party, or any special interest in the Order, whose purpose and function in the communion seemed to him too obviously artificial, not a response to a real need, Ernest was sorry. At Holy Trinity they were not numerous enough to make one man, more or less, of no importance. They hadn't the tradition or assurance to suffer easily the loss of this particular one, so long their most popular and effective preacher—the member of the Order best known to their public. He put the letter on the stand, saw the pad on which he had started to write last night.

The telephone directory proved to be under the bed, along with a pair of slippers, one black shoe, a clerical collar, and a several weeks' old copy of the *Churchman*. It must be the one with that letter of Wilber's. He fished it out and threw it into the armchair across the room. Cradling the telephone, he sat back, crossed his bare hairy shins and searched the directory pages.

The number was rung some time, and she said, "Hello," so dazedly that it was plain that he had awakened her.

"Geraldine," he said. "Good morning, my dear. How do you feel?"

"Oh, Ernie—well, I don't know. Awful, I guess."

"Get some coffee. I wouldn't take anything else. A friend of mine is going with you. Have you something to write on? Put down this address—" He repeated it to her. "Be there at ten o'clock, and ask for Mrs. Breen. I think you'll like her. She'll take you over to the doctor—I have every reason to believe, a good and skillful one—a woman."

"All right," she said faintly, and paused. "You didn't tell him, did you? I don't want him to know."

"I haven't told him."

"I don't want him to find out. I don't want him to come anywhere near me. You won't let him, will you?" Her breath caught and she began, though stiffly, as if still numb with sleep, to cry. "I don't want him to get drunk, or something, and come up here."

"I won't let him. The doctor probably won't send you home for a few days. No one else will know where you are. Now, don't cry. There's nothing to cry about."

"I wish I didn't have to do it. I feel so awful, as if I were going to die. Ernie, what shall I do?"

Ernest lit another cigarette. "What you must do is be a brave girl. Make some coffee. Get dressed. Go over there. I'll come and see you late this afternoon."

"Will you?"

"Of course. God bless you, Geraldine."

There was a tap on the door. "Come!" he called.

"Good morning, Vicar." It was Mr. Johnston. His bleak face was freshly shaved. He looked bright and cheerful. "Oh, I beg your pardon," he said, seeing the telephone still in Ernest's hands. "I've just rung off," Ernest said.

"Oh! I'm glad I didn't interrupt you. I—er—wondered if you could find a minute sometime about my sermon tomorrow. I thought—er—if you had time—I don't want to trouble you."

"Sit down. Tell me about it."

"Well, it came to me from the Gospel for last Sunday— the miraculous draught of fishes, you know—"

The telephone rang. "Sorry," Ernest said. "Yes?"

"Hello, darling."

"Thank goodness you called me. I don't know your Harriet's last name, so I couldn't call you. Mrs. Binney—

she's called Geraldine—will be over. She's a nice kid. You can handle her. I don't think she'd better be sent home. Doubtless your friend knows some private hospital. Better put her there. Ring me later. Oh, and get her sister's address from her."

"Well, maybe I'd better bring my manuscript," Mr. Johnston whispered. He arose and moved on tiptoe toward the door.

"Do," Ernest said.

Alice said, "All right. Afterward you might take me to lunch."

"My dear, Heaven knows when I'll be free. I may not have time for lunch."

"Find time, Ernie. I think I'm going to divorce Lee. I want to talk to you. I didn't get a chance last night."

"I don't think you're going to do anything of the sort. And if you are, I strongly disapprove. You'd better call him at the hotel and find out what happened to him. To-morrow you can both come to dinner here, if you want to."

"No. I want to see you before I see him."

"Very well, if you don't mind waiting until I can get away. I can tell you definitely later— Yes," he said. "Come! Hello, Carl. Sit down— Call the Chapel House, Alice. I'll be over there."

He put the telephone back on the stand, picked up the letter from Holy Trinity, and tossed it to Carl.

"Father Cudlipp, eh?" Carl said. "Of the Anglican Obedience?"

Ernest's pajamas were much too small for him. They wrinkled up almost to his knees and elbows. They strained open on his full white chest and started back on his rounded shoulders. The unsparing sunlight, poured on the armchair, made him look older than he had appeared the night before. His once dense curly black hair had thinned on top to show the pale scalp through it. His features, always a trifle snub, but, once, almost romantically handsome, had suffered a certain thickening. His cheeks, under the short stubble of beard, were florid and young-colored, but they had a loose fullness bound to end in jowls.

"Stupid old man!" Carl snorted, throwing the letter back. "That's like him. He's just an endless gush of goodness. In the old days, I often used to have to hot-foot it over to chapel—a kind of spiritual trots—and pray fervently that I wouldn't hurt God's feelings by socking His faithful servant in the benign puss."

"I thought it a creditable letter," said Ernest. "Why don't you go back, Carl? At your age and mine, one's too old to learn a new trade."

"Is that your reason for all this?" He jerked out a hand to indicate the Vicarage. "Well, I suppose it's a living. Then, of course, there's that pie in the sky, if and when issued."

"What are you trying to do, Carl?" asked Ernest. "Get me started on a defense of Christian doctrine, so that you can have some fun with it?" He smiled. "You're a much abler theologian than I am. I'm not likely to lecture you in your subject. And you ought to know that I'm certainly not going to argue with you, anyway. Don't be childish! Why not stop all this and tell me about the real trouble?"

"So you don't know?"

"I have an idea."

"You're pretty smart." The jauntiness, the airiness, which he assumed was disagreeable; but you had to make some allowance for Carl's habit of mind or emotion. "Nobody up there had." He said it as though he despised the dupes at Holy Trinity for their denseness; yet, at the same time, complimented himself for a wonderfully sustained and skillful hypocrisy.

Ernest found it very doubtful. To a mind like Carl's everything must be rendered in excess—black as hell, bright as Heaven. Carl's sins could not be less than scarlet; and if he fell, he would take care to fall like Lucifer. A single lapse dissatisfied him. He would have to imply that for years he had been wallowing in secret sin.

"Last week," Carl said, "the police of a certain city felt obliged to let the cat out of the bag. I was coming back from a mission. I happened to be short of money, or I daresay I could have fixed it."

"Was it in the papers?"

"Oh, no." He became elaborately vivacious. "That has its amusing side. At the police station the captain was, naturally, a good R.C. Naturally, too, he'd never heard of an Anglican religious order. Poor man, he thought he was dealing with the True Church, and if he didn't watch his step, he'd go to hell. I had to laugh—"

Now, certainly, Carl was lying. It wasn't hard, it wasn't pleasant, to picture that scene in the police station. "Go on," said Ernest.

"Being, in short," Carl said, "a just man, and not willing to make me a public example, he was minded to put me away privily. So he telephoned the monastery. It wasn't the easiest thing in the world to explain on the telephone, but he did it with rare delicacy. His plain-clothes agent provocateur, who'd picked me up, hoping I might have fifty dollars, was sadly set down. He had to put me on a train. No charges, no unfortunate publicity, no scandal to edify the ungodly! And all due to sound early training by the Sisters at the parochial school. I never really appreciated Rome before."

"I see," said Ernest. "What happened at Holy Trinity?"

"Great excitement," Carl said. "Give me a cigarette, will you? They called the brethren in from near and far. How to hush it up? Old Father Cowles was so overcome that he kept having to go out and weep bitterly. Father Howard, who was my confessor, was at his wit's end for a suitable penance. I think he was pondering Origen's clam shell. Father Superior wished to spend the night praying with me before the Blessed Sacrament—"

The door swung open.

"Oh, I beg your pardon!" Mr. Johnston backed out precipitately. "I'll see you later, Vicar. I didn't know—"

"Leave the manuscript," said Ernest. "I'll take it over to the office with me. We'll get at it sometime this afternoon. If you have time, find out about Mrs. Hawley, will you? I'd rely more on what the doctor says than on what she says, by the way. She sometimes exaggerates. But I'll get over if it's really serious."

"Yes. I meant to do that, Vicar. I'll go at once."

"Think he was getting an earful?" asked Carl.

"I know he wasn't. He's one of the few people I've ever met who is altogether without guile. Go on."

"That's the end of it. After two days of their weeping and wailing, I was fed up. I told them to go to hell. I was sick of their pretenses and maudlin cant. What I'd done, I'd done. If they thought I was penitent, they were crazy."

"I'm surprised it took you two days," Ernest said. But it was surprising only in the light of the story Carl had now made of it. It would be safe to assume that he behaved very differently—wept bitterly with Father Cowles; had hysterics with Father Howard in the confessional; prayed all night with the Father Superior, before the exhaustion of his nerves, and his natural knack for dramatizing himself, made him reverse his rôle, embrace the horror, be frankly the damned soul that his lively imagination made him sure he was. Another reversal was clearly not out of the question.

"They wouldn't let me go," Carl said. "It's harder to return to the world than you think. You have no clothes. You have no money." He shrugged. "I'd thought I might as well go back there and face it. I went back. I faced it. Don't think it's easy for me to—"

"I don't think it's easy."

Ernest didn't. He thought, if anything, that Carl himself made too little of the difficulty of returning to the world—was returning the word, when one had never, as an adult, been there at all? He doubted if Carl had formed any calm idea of what the things he was giving up meant to him, and suddenly he remembered that Sunday dinner in Florence.

It was a very good and pleasant dinner. The rector of Saint James' was a young man of cordial charm, at once worldly and charitable, with an urbane continental experience and a rich, cheerful wife. Father Willever was the life of that party—eager, gay; even witty. Really he radiated a kind of love. He loved everyone. He distributed his attention with a loving, tender interest. In effect, he took each of them by the arm, urged each, gently, irresistibly, to rejoice with him; for that morning he had labored more abundantly than they all; yet not he—he was winning, in a humility which does not offend by assertion, being simply there, and felt—but the grace of God which was with him. Across the table Ernest could see the Father Superior's severe, rather crusty, long-nosed face as he lifted his wine glass, sipped abstemiously. Stiffly he smirked at Ernest with the ingenuous self-congratulation of an old man who has a good son, if only in Christ.

"I've written some people," Carl said. "I'll write some more, if you have a pen and ink."

"Don't write too many people."

Carl looked at him. "Why not?"

"Because it's none of their business."

"They'll find out sooner or later."

"Let it be later," said Ernest. "You can stay here as long as you want, and I think that's what you'd better do. Come over to the Chapel House about one, and we'll eat somewhere."

"I thought I heard you making a luncheon date when I came downstairs."

"Now you hear me break it—" He smiled. "Carl, you look much better this morning. We'll work this out."

The telephone rang and he reached for it. It was Bill Jennings from the office. "Yes, I'm coming," Ernest said. "Well, he can call later. Yes, I know. I don't care what Miss Thomas said. Miss Thomas is mistaken. If you see Joe, tell him not to go away. I want him to explain to me why there was no hot water in the gymnasium shower rooms Wednesday night."

Carl said, "You haven't anything I could shave with, have you?"

Ernest went into the bathroom and gave Carl his razor. For himself, he could borrow John's.

John's room was shadowed and silent in that false, unconvincing order of things placed neatly to cover as much of a fundamental dirt and confusion as possible. Lily resorted to it when the weather was warm or her disposition surly.

Pinned casually to the wall by the bureau was a charcoal drawing which Ernest had not noticed when he brought Lulu in there last night. In spirited caricature, its figures were fitted to the circular shape of a conventionalized, medieval Trinity. The Father sat enthroned, a gross jovial man, a smug Santa Claus in the lawn sleeves of a bishop.

He wore a top hat tilted back until its brim was something like a halo. Between his knees stood the Son, a little boy with a beard clad in a scout uniform. The Father's hand held, indulgently, as if it were a dove, a radio microphone.

Ernest was obliged to laugh. He pulled the sheet from its thumb tacks, took it to the desk, and picking up a pencil, scribbled on the back: *I've seen it. You can put it away now. E.C.* He moved a paperweight onto it and went back to the bureau.

John's pigskin toilet kit was not in sight. Nor was it in the top drawer. He turned over the jumble of silk socks, collars for dress shirts, and initialed handkerchiefs. There was nothing under them but a large photograph. In a dramatic rich dusk of shadow the face of a thin, pretty-eyed girl with short fluffy hair looked up at him from the bottom of the drawer. She had written on it: *John, with passionate sincerity*—he could not make out the name. It looked like *Alix*. Ernest shot the drawer shut, the tolerant, almost affectionate mood in which he had scribbled on the back of the drawing gone. Plainly it was the young woman at Joseph's last night. "He must be taking up with schoolgirls!" Ernest said. He went out to see if he could find Mr. Johnston's razor.

What he had hoped of John couldn't be briefly or neatly put. Ernest supposed that it was the general paternal hope, the fond urgent wish for every good thing to be John's. He would have hoped, he supposed, that as years passed he would see John develop into a person of character, intelligent and responsible, master of the simple secret of a good, happy and fruitful life. What, in particular, he would be, necessarily depended on John's own abilities; but, at least, into his forties, he would not be like Lee Breen, vain, captious, and childish; nor could he, like Carl Willever, find himself suddenly overmastered by who knew what degrading and ruinous impulse.

Exasperated, Ernest thought: "I won't have it! I'm not going to let him go on this way. If I can't handle a spoiled brat—"

His anger was still bright and hot, but he felt better, as though he had already cuffed some of the conceit out of John, and seen miraculously restored the diffidence, the earnest intellectual aspirations, the simple enthusiasms of the youth who used to come down from school; even, of the one who showed off with such transparent hope for his approval only a year or so ago in long literary letters from college.

——— • ———

The Chapel and the Vicarage faced north. Backed up close to the Chapel, facing south on the other street, was the somber, red brick, Romanesque pile of the Chapel House. It was about forty years old. Built against it on the far side, eloquently demonstrating the change in architectural taste effected in so short a time was the clean functional glass and concrete of the new building which housed Holy Innocents' Dispensary, and the parish's day nursery.

Ernest went out in the blaze of sun in the backyard of the Vicarage, through the gate and along the side of the Chapel, and so into the heavy cool gloom of the lower hall in the Chapel House. From the locker rooms and basketball court to his right there was a stronger than usual pungence of sweat, urine, and musty old gymnasium mats. His steps echoed with him up the iron stairs, past the cramped and gloomy auditorium; on up, and into the Vicar's office.

Bill Jennings sat at the battered drophead desk with the typewriter in the corner, scratching his head. He turned a clear, dumb, honest face. On a straight-backed chair in the other corner sat the janitor—he was called the Chief Engineer—a lean, melancholy man with an air of bitter authority so necessary in dealing with mischief-makers, destroyers of Chapel House property, and outsiders who had no business there. Despite the efforts of Wilber Quinn and Mr. Plummer, the part-time sports director, Joe was known to most of the boys as Steel Balls and frequently addressed that way. Ernest suspected that Joe considered it a compliment.

"That hot water furnace, now, Mr. Cudlipp," he began at once. "It's no good. I've patched it every way I know. Even had a plumber see it. Looks like we got to buy a new one. Though cold water don't hurt the boys any I can see."

"It's the only bath lots of them ever get," said Ernest, taking up the heap of mail on the roll-top desk. "Soap and hot water seem to me essential. Bill, call that new Superintendent of Buildings at the Parish House and ask him to come over. Just a moment, Joe. I had another note from Miss Thomas yesterday complaining that their garbage cans hadn't been taken out. What's wrong with Frank? Drunk again?"

"I doubt if he's touched a drop since that time last Christmas, Mr. Cudlipp," Joe said bitterly. After all, Frank was his brother-in-law. "He was sick yesterday. He went home."

"Next time he's sick he's not to go home until he has reported to the Dispensary. I want Doctor Fowler, or Doctor Casali, to be able to tell me what made him sick. And any work he doesn't do, you'll have to do. We can't have friction with Miss Thomas or her organization. That building isn't in my charge, so we want to be particularly careful to do the things we're supposed to do for them when they're supposed to be done."

"The thing is, there's no satisfying her, Mr. Cudlipp. She's a fault-finder. She looks until she finds it. I told her that. I told her—"

"Well, I hope you'll never tell her that again. We can't get along if you're going to talk to her that way. Do what she asks, and if you feel it's not work you should do, tell me afterward. I'll see that you aren't required to do it again."

"Now, don't you worry about it, Mr. Cudlipp. I didn't mean it was anything serious—just a matter of nag, nag, nag. I understand it. She's suffering from change of life, and it affects some women that way. Can't be helped."

"That seems to me very likely," said Ernest, "but I don't think the subject needs discussion. Go down and do what you can about the lavatory in the boys' locker room. It smells."

Left alone with Bill Jennings, he said, "About Jimmy. If they've got nothing on him but what you told me, we might get him off. But this would be the last time. What's his trouble, Bill?"

Bill Jennings shifted in his chair. "I don't know, Mr. Cudlipp. Nothing has any effect on him. Pa's licked him until he couldn't sit down. I've tried to talk to him. I got him to come over here and try for the basketball team, and he did for a while; and I know Mr. Quinn talked to him. He don't—he doesn't care. What can you do with a person like that? It isn't any use telling him what he does is wrong. He just laughs at you." He looked at Ernest, harassed and doubtful. "It's an awful thing to say about your own brother, Mr. Cudlipp; but I got to admit, if it was anybody else's brother, I'd say in jail was just where he ought to be. I know plenty about him. If it wasn't for Pa, that is. He feels terrible."

"I'll try to get down to the station at noon and have a talk with someone." Ernest took up a flat sealed package.

"That came by messenger from the Parish House," Bill said. He seemed more relieved than not to close the discussion about Jimmy. "He said it was the page proof for the year book. Miss Stoddard wanted you should telephone her right away, if there was any more corrections in your report, because the printer has to have it this afternoon." He propped up the stenographic notebook beside him and began to type.

The cut sheets of flimsy paper were bound without a cover. In celebration of the 100th Anniversary, the year book had been made much more elaborate than usual—octavo, with a special hand-set type. Each article and report began with a big inset blank square which was to be filled by an illuminated initial. Thirty photographs, mostly of the new church and its beautiful detail, had been leafed in.

The frontispiece was an old engraving of the first church, downtown. The building was small and unpretentious, but it had a good spire and perfect proportions. The architect was unknown, probably because the builder himself had prepared any plans he needed. He must have been an intelligent man with an instinctive feeling for modifications of the Colonial tradition in the neo-classic Federalist taste. How anyone who ever worshiped in that first Holy Innocents' could have endured the second church—a senseless jumble of fake Gothic, erected two miles farther uptown—was one of those mysteries in which the true course and meaning of civilization doubtless hid. It wasn't as if they had never seen a decent and dignified building. They had. They possessed and used such a building. Yet, in 1873, they left it, actually with thanksgiving, for the monstrosity whose picture faced page twenty—

"Oh, Mr. Cudlipp," said Bill, scratching his ear, "were you going to call Mr. Shevlin?"

"Mr. Shevlin? Oh—certainly not. If he wants to continue that discussion, he'll have to call me. Well, wait a minute. See if you can get Miss Thomas on the phone. We may as well understand each other."

There was some delay and Ernest picked up a pencil, began to run down through the paragraphs of the Vicar's Report. "Mr. Cudlipp calling," said Bill. Ernest took the telephone from him, rocked back in the shaky swivel chair. "Good morning, Miss Thomas," he said. "I've just been speaking to Joe about the garbage cans. I don't think it will happen again. I'm sorry it did happen."

She said, "Well, I'm sorry, too, Mr. Cudlipp. It wasn't by any means the first time, you know—"

She went on to make some general observations about Joe and Joe's work, so Ernest rocked forward, took up the pencil and began again on the proof. "Yes," he said, "I know that does happen sometimes." He struck out an extra "c" in ecumenical. "Yes. Yes. Yes." He turned the page and reached for a cigarette in the flat tin box on the desk.

"Yes," he said; "well, he mustn't do that. Now, Miss Thomas, what about some people named Shevlin? He seems to be unemployed, and I'm told it's general knowledge in the neighborhood that he's one of those people on Relief who won't take work. His wife had some sort of part-time job and there are three small children. They're Roman Catholics. Somebody sent them around to me and I told them that the day nursery wouldn't be open to them. Apparently they then went to you. Do you remember about it?"

"Yes. They're relatives of Miss Mead's."

Miss Mead was the dietitian. "Well, then, of course you told them that it was impossible."

"On the contrary, I told them that we'd take the children. Miss Mead had explained about them to me—"

Ernest began to read again, but inattentively. It was really astounding. Perhaps, by herself explaining at such length, Miss Thomas showed that she was conscious of an explanation being badly needed; but that consciousness wouldn't keep her from trying to do her favorite, Miss Mead, a favor. It was really an occupational disease, endemic among social service workers. Just as the people they worked with soon came to regard things given them or done for them as no more—indeed, a little less—than their inalienable right, the distributers of the largess soon stopped seeing themselves as officers administering a trust. The funds and facilities put at their disposal became, if not their own property, at least their prerogative. The money was there. Somebody was going to get it. So why not those whom they personally liked and favored?

"Miss Thomas, we can't do it," Ernest said. "As you know, we have to make an absolute rule. These people are parishioners of Father Maloney's—or would be, if they went to church at all. I have to tell them that unless Father Maloney will send me his written permission, we won't take the children. Of course he can't do anything of the sort. They're strictly forbidden to bring their children here."

"That doesn't change the fact that they live in the neighborhood, and that the children aren't properly cared for at home. I see no reason why we shouldn't take them."

"There are three reasons," Ernest said patiently. "First, we aren't doing any proselyting among Father Maloney's people. Especially not of the sort which they used to call 'souperism' in the old country. It would lead to a great deal of bitterness and misunderstanding. Second, we have our hands full, these days—the year's report happens to be in front of me, and I wonder if you know how full they are—with our own Chapel people. Third, the last case in which we could properly make an exception would be one involving relatives of a member of the staff."

"I have already told them that they may come."

"Well, you shouldn't have done it, Miss Thomas. It puts

118

you in an embarrassing position, since they can't be admitted unless their admission cards are countersigned. I'm not going to countersign them."

"I shall take the matter to Doctor Lamb."

"That would be your best course. If he countersigns the cards, there'll be no further difficulty."

"I'm perfectly aware of that. Good morning."

"Good morning," said Ernest.

To Bill he said, "Well, I botched it! But why didn't you tell me that they were relatives of Miss Mead's? I might have done better if I hadn't been so taken by surprise. I don't like that sort of thing around here. Well, Doctor Lamb would like it no better. I doubt if she calls him when she's thought it over. So something is accomplished."

"I hate her," Bill said simply. "So does everybody, I guess; except, maybe, Miss Mead, and some people like that."

"I practically asked for it," said Ernest, "but that doesn't make the feeling one to be encouraged. If what you guess is true, it might help you to think more charitably of her if you imagined how you would feel if everyone hated you. It's much more than punishment enough."

"Oh, sure," said Bill. "I guess she's all right. She kind of gripes people, that's all—"

Ernest closed the subject by returning to the proof. He was habitually a little too candid with Bill—a type of imprudence you could be sure of regretting sooner or later. Bill's devotion to him needn't be questioned; but devotion was no substitute for judgment.

Ernest read at random: *In July, Saint Ambrose's Camp opened for the thirty-second season. During the first two weeks, the Vicar was in residence with seventy-five boys. For the second two weeks, Mr. Maury, of the Church Staff, took charge of sixty-two girls—*

And didn't get on very well with them, either. They were a tough crowd—much tougher than anything Mr. Maury, a recently ordained young man, had ever encountered before. Probably the experience had been instructive, for the girls were (as far as good judges could conveniently determine) good girls—the pick of the lot. Mr. Maury couldn't have helped seeing how little he was fitted to deal with the material over here, even when it was, relatively, as promising as possible. All the camp girls had attended Sunday school for a number of years; many of them were confirmed; and those old enough to face a choice in the matter were at least making an effort to be virtuous. Mr. Maury had tried to treat them as he had so successfully treated the Saturday Morning Club over at Holy Innocents'—a group made up entirely of private school girls who enjoyed an active and varied program of creative dancing, swimming, and basketball.

Mr. Maury needn't feel too discouraged. Ernest hoped he didn't, for the general genius of the Church had a great deal more to do with the girls he met Saturday morning than with those who peopled his nightmare down at the camp. Saint Ambrose's Chapel was all very well, and might be said to have done great good in its time, yet really no good so great as the good it did Holy Innocents' soul. Essentially, the Chapel was Holy Innocents' answer to the lesson of the Good Samaritan. So amply forewarned, they didn't pass by on the other side. They were looking for chances to stop. Their compassion was real. They were acutely distressed to hear of the poor and miserable. Although, in fact, the poverty and misery around the Chapel was not extreme, it was terrible enough to them. They got down and tried to bind up the wounds. They, too, poured in oil and wine, anxiously illustrating the new parable of the Good Levite.

The telephone rang. "Mr. Johnston," Bill announced, handing it to him. Mr. Johnston, stammering slightly, said, "Oh, Vicar, I'm at the Hawleys'. Would it be possible for you to come over?"

"You mean right now?"

"Well, yes. If you can arrange it. I think it is grave. And a problem has arisen with which I don't feel competent to deal. I hope I'm not inconveniencing you."

"No. I'll come." He said to Bill, "Will you go to the bank and cash a check for me? If it isn't done before noon, I won't be able to get any money—"

He stirred up the contents of the top drawer until he found a check book. The last four or five stubs were not filled in, so he had no idea what his balance was, except that it was bound to be low. "Ten dollars," he said. "No, it'll have to be fifteen. I owe Wilber five. All right. I oughtn't to be more than half an hour."

———— • ————

Ernest went down the Chapel House steps onto the sunny side of the street. The pavement was crowded with people who moved laboriously in the heat. Men loading or unloading trucks backed to the curb held the stream up. Women dragged along with marketing bags, stopped without warning to stare into the small shop windows. Ernest, hatless, picked his way briskly through the sluggish press. Many people, seeing his bare head and clerical collar, looked at him again, amazed. The majority of them probably lived within a block or so of the Chapel, but they had not the faintest idea who he was, why he was dressed that way, or what he was doing here.

Rounding the corner Ernest passed into shadow along the elevated, by comparison cool and refreshing. Half way down the block he came to a fish store whose windows displayed some eels and a few limp flounders lying on beds of broken ice. Beyond it, the sidewalk was half covered with trestles and stands spread solid with vegetables which a clerk was sprinkling with a watering pot. Between the two, Ernest identified the Hawleys' door by the worn gilt and black sign, *Roomers.*

Mr. Hawley still owned, though precariously, the building—the vegetable dealers were his tenants. As far as the neighborhood and the Chapel congregation went, Mr. Hawley would have been, in so-called normal times, what passed for prosperous—and what must still pass for that, reflected Ernest, remembering his thoughts in the office only a few minutes ago.

If this looked squalid compared to what one found a few blocks, a quarter mile, west, would any word serve for the things you could see two miles south—or two miles north, for that matter?

Two miles south would be the district around Saint Matthew's old Parish House. Ernest thought of it. During his first year as Doctor Ogilvie's curate he had lived there, come and gone through the desolate filthy streets. Saint Matthew's, which had lost, first by its inconvenience, then by Doctor Ogilvie's peculiar régime, many of the old families who once supported it, had neither the funds nor the equipment to make the slightest impression on these surroundings. Saint Matthew's, the fine, historic church, simply stood, grimy, gracefully aloof, in the plot of garden left from the fields of the eighteenth century. Ernest had been obliged to carry a key to the great oak doors of the Parish House, for they were always kept locked. People then living in what had once been the parish would not be likely to come there except to look for something to steal.

Ernest went in the Hawleys' door and up the stairs. Facing him at the top was a neat, ugly parlor. Elaborate curtains shadowed it. It was decorated with too many very large stupid pictures in even larger oak frames. A number of little stands supported ferns growing in pots. Among them Mr. Johnston sat, the deep wrinkles of his face folded in a sad, anxious vacancy. When he saw Ernest, he jerked to his feet and came toward him. He said in an intense whisper, as though he were giving directions to an acolyte at the altar, "The doctor came just a moment ago. I had a word with him before he went in to see her. It's very grave, I fear. I think he's quite changed his idea—"

An elevated train passed. Mr. Johnston's mouth moved soundless in the grinding roar. When it had faded he proved to be saying "—I took a partial medical course many years ago at McGill, you know. It was at Hudson Stuck's suggestion. He was quite right. It was invaluable to me." His agitation overcame him and he stuttered a moment. "Not that I'm in any way qualified to be a physician, or to venture an opinion to one. It would be very wrong of me to give that impression." He pressed a shaking hand to his shabby gray hair. "You see, Mrs. Hawley is convinced that she suffers from cancer. She thinks that there is one of those common conspiracies to deceive her about it, that the doctor is not telling her the truth. In fact, he was in error. When I first saw her, I could not help wondering. I did not think it would be proper to make suggestions—"

"You mean that it is cancer, then?" Ernest asked.

"No, no. I wouldn't know about that. The doctor finally received a report from an analysis of her water and I think it's quite clearly a form of acute parenchymatous hepatitis, an—er—decomposition of the liver. I believe I may be more familiar with it than he is. It's not so very common in civilization; but, it happens, that many Indian women die of it during the—er—puerperium. A physician at Skagway diagnosed it for me."

"I see."

"Yes. One doesn't know quite what to do, whether she should be told."

"I don't think I follow you," Ernest said.

"Oh, well, you see, believing she has a cancer, which a sister of hers appears to have had, she is much depressed, and expects to die. But having nursed a case, she does not expect to die at once." His magnified eyes swam anxiously toward Ernest. "Ought she to be told that she is, in fact, dying now? There is no hope whatsoever. The liver simply breaks up. Doubtless it has already largely disappeared. The next stage is delirium and hallucinations. How much longer she will remain in her right mind is a question. She will die in a comatose state tomorrow, or the next day at latest. Ought she to have an opportunity to prepare for it?"

"I don't think it essential," said Ernest. "Unless there is strong reason to suppose that it would be a comfort to her. What particular reason did she have for wanting to see me?"

"Why, I'm afraid it was I who thought it advisable," Mr. Johnston said in embarrassment. "I don't know it from her, but her husband has told me that she was baptized a Roman Catholic. She said something to him. I think it possible that—"

"I see," said Ernest.

"Yes, yes," Mr. Johnston nodded. "What do you advise? I thought that if you could talk to her—unfortunately, I am still practically a stranger to her—you could make her see better than I could that it is not a matter of the rites of some particular church. After all, she has been for most of her life, I understand, a communicant of ours. I—er— took the precaution of bringing with me the little traveling case I have, thinking she might wish to receive Holy Communion. But she said not, and I fear it is connected with

124

this matter—" He turned, hearing footsteps. "That's the doctor now," he said. "Do you know him?"

"Yes, I do."

"Oh, but of course you do!" said Mr. Johnston. "Better than I do! It's Doctor Casali, from the clinic. How stupid of me!"

Ernest had no more than a speaking acquaintance with him. Doctor Casali was about thirty. He managed his wiry, undersized body self-consciously. He kept his chin, even at his age blue-shadowed from a beard too stubborn and persistent for shaving to conceal for more than an hour or two, pulled in at a point of visible strain. He threw his little chest out belligerently, staring hard and critical around him. It gave him an air of hoping by an insolent manner to add the needed cubit to his stature. He looked at Ernest as though about to reprimand him and said in his low, but harsh, assertive voice: "Good morning."

"Good morning," Ernest answered. "Can anything be done for her?"

"I'm going over for some morphine," Doctor Casali said. "No sense in anything else." Plainly he intended to include, if his hearers chose to take it that way, what ministrations they might contemplate. "Someone ought to stay with her. I can't. I have a hundred things to do this morning."

"Does she know?"

"I should think so." Doctor Casali gave him a moderately contemptuous stare. "She may not know what it is, but she knows all she needs to. If you expect to see her, better do it now. When I come back, I want to put her under; and we may as well keep her there." He went on downstairs.

"That young man impresses me unfavorably," Ernest

said. "I'm glad I have no responsibility for the clinic. I'd have trouble being fair to him."

"Oh, I believe he's competent. He's very well informed, I know. His manner seems a little brusque; but I suppose he means nothing by it."

"What he means by it is that he hasn't forgiven his parents for begetting him and bringing him up in a slum. He means that he hasn't forgiven the people at his medical school who cold-shouldered him because he was poor and vulgar and didn't dress properly. He means he hasn't forgiven the people who, with half his ability, had the pull to get good appointments. He means he isn't forgiving Holy Innocents' for being able to hire him to do work of this sort, instead of whatever work he may want to do."

"How unfortunate! You've known him for some time, then?"

"No. I'm simply guessing. What I know are the symptoms. It's his misfortune, not his fault. So I wish I could find him less objectionable. I can't. I've tried. That's my misfortune."

Mr. Johnston was listening uncomfortably, not able to agree with him, not wishing to seem to disagree. Mr. Johnston had a right to be pained. The teachings of his faith, as he understood them, would forbid him such a prejudice. It would be possible to imagine Mr. Johnston, simply and naturally in his nervous, diffident way, performing the sublime moral feat of distinguishing between the hatred of abomination and the hatred of enmity. With purest benevolence, he could probably manage to hate quietly any bad deed; yet love, as he was bound to love all his fellow men, the doer. "It's my misfortune," repeated Ernest. "Well, I'd better see her. Is Mr. Hawley there?"

"Er—he went out for a moment." Mr. Johnston coughed doubtfully. "I'm sorry to say that I think he is drinking. Even as early as this, I could smell spirits on his breath. But if it gives him any comfort, it seems hard to blame him—"

"It's a good excuse to get down a little," Ernest said. "I daresay he thinks he needs it. He has a slight tendency to need it now and then. But, need it or not, he can't be allowed to go off on a bat unless it's arranged that someone will stay with her."

"Yes, of course. She mustn't be left alone," Mr. Johnston said. "I'd be very glad to stay with her, if you thought you could spare me, Vicar. It would perhaps be easier for me. Her condition would be bound to distress anyone to whom she was near and dear. Particularly a person without medical experience—I mean, one who has seen little sickness. Well, whatever you think."

Ernest went forward along the short hall, tapped on the closed door at the end, and opened it quietly. In the shadow of the drawn blinds, which swayed occasionally over two inches of window open under them, the room was warmer than the hall—close, dim, definitely fetid.

Exactly on a level with the windows an elevated train went uptown, steel wheels screaming over the steel track perhaps fifteen yards from Mrs. Hawley on the bed. Although she had heard the door open, she did not seem to hear the train. Trains had passed like that for years and she no longer noticed them.

Ernest walked directly to the tarnished brass bedstead. He said as cheerfully as he could: "Well, Mrs. Hawley. I'm extremely sorry to see you ill."

She answered him with a great groan. The conventional, experimental remark, given a response so shocking, became absurd. The body on the bed wanted no name or title. Ernest's extreme sorrow was a form of speech only, for hers was the extreme sorrow and it was wordless. She declared it, stertorous; a sound compounded, as she groaned, retched, hawked, strangling in an expression beyond speech.

Ernest sat down on a shabby cane-bottomed chair, leaned forward, his elbows on his knees, looking at her. "What would you like me to do, Mrs. Hawley?" he asked.

She shook her head, though not necessarily in answer; for, frenzied, she twisted it so that it fell first on one cheek, then, wildly thrown over, on the other. Her hands, clenched on the wrinkled sheet, were buried in the full pit of her stomach. Groaning, she became again motionless.

After a moment her eyelids parted. She looked wavering at Ernest in the shadow, then past him. The glazed whites showed blind with a lacquered shine like patent leather against the deep dirty yellow of her ravaged face. Under the sheet—her body bending, her knees drawing up—a slow involuntary spasm doubled her. Her head rolled back and forth. She groaned deep, again and again, as fast as she could. At the corners of her mouth appeared a slight, stained, bubbling slime. The lips contracted, moved as though talking. Downtown roared an elevated train, so if she said anything, it could not be heard.

Ernest stood up and went to the door. "Mr. Johnston," he said. Mr. Johnston had been standing aimlessly at the head of the stairs. He came up in loose, awkward haste. "Come in," said Ernest. "I want you to see if you think she's conscious."

Mr. Johnston bent his angular form over the bed. He peered at her. He removed his glasses, staring and frowning closer. "Do you hear me?" he said.

She groaned once more. Looking at Ernest he said, "She does." He replaced his glasses. Gently, his hand shaking a little, he took the edge of the sheet, wiped the corners of her mouth. In a hoarse whisper, he went on: "I wonder if perhaps she should not be given the Sacrament? Of course, it's a question if she could keep it down—"

Ernest was unable to do more than look at him.

Turning again to her, Mr. Johnston said: "Mrs. Hawley, Jesus is near. He knows. He hears. Won't you speak to Him?" He looked back at Ernest. "I'm not easy about her—her state of mind," he said. "It's a question what to do— There!" he said. "There!" He stroked her forehead.

"I see only one thing to do about that," Ernest said. "We'd better do it. Have you a nickel? I have no change."

Mr. Johnston fumbled in his pocket until he found the coin. Ernest took it into the hall. Leaning against the wall, he dropped it into the slot of the pay telephone there. "Information," he said.

Mr. Johnston came tiptoeing out into the hall, too; looked at him, made a gesture, probably of apology, tiptoed back. Ernest said: "Get me the rectory, or any telephone connection there is, at the Roman Catholic Church of Saint Andrew Corsini. Oh, it's only a few blocks from here. I don't recall the exact address. Find it, please."

The door below banged. Up the stairs came careful, ponderous steps. Ernest's eyes, fixed on the bannisters of the short rail, saw between them Mr. Hawley's beefy face lifting into view. He looked at Ernest, then looked away again, mounting doggedly. At the top he looked once more at Ernest and Ernest pointed to the open parlor door.

Mr. Hawley stared, his light eyes blank and sorrowful in his crimson face, started to turn and go toward Mrs. Hawley's room. Ernest shook his head. "Go in there," he said. "I want to talk to you. Oh, excuse me. Is Father Maloney there, or do you know where he can be reached? It's Mr. Cudlipp, of Saint Ambrose's Chapel."

Putting his hand over the mouthpiece, Ernest lifted his eyebrows and said to Mr. Hawley, who still stood irresolute, "I want to see you! I'll be through here in a moment. Wait." Removing his hand, he said, "Father Maloney? Mr. Cudlipp. I have here a very sick woman. I find that she was brought up one of your people. She has been a member of our congregation for many years, but I think she would like to die in your communion. Will you help her?"

"Hm," said Father Maloney. "Ah! Well, now, Mr. Cudlipp, do you yourself know personally that she's a Catholic? She hasn't any record of her baptism, has she?"

His tones, so inevitable, so like his appearance, made Father Maloney practically present. Ernest saw his pale solid face, moony and luminous; the soft full neck, one single slanting line from the point of his chin to the edge of his collar. In the least cough or throat-clearing sounded the unique, peculiar air of authority and condescension; the bureaucratic, to Ernest not very agreeable, everyday voice of Rome, which went so naturally with the power of the keys.

As a matter of fact, Father Maloney supported the awful presumption well. If anything marred his dignity, it was a certain unnecessary overassurance. Ernest supposed that it was an inheritance, the enduring contribution of the little boy who, early destined for the priesthood, found that he took precedence over his brothers and sisters, even over his parents (*Wist ye not that I must be about my Father's business?*). At the seminary they, of course, corrected personal conceit; but they taught him at the same time the full meaning of his consecration. He was given no reason to think a priest anything less than he might have judged as a child from the servilely pious old women ducking, flustered by the Father's visit; or from the uncertain, slightly shamefaced reverence sooner or later enforced on no matter how manly and ribald a street corner sinner.

For once, the child's daydream triumphed in the man's experience and Father Maloney kept a trace of the little dreamer's innocent, irritating presumption, aged now into a permanent, if hardly noticeable, defect in breeding.

"Hello, hello," Father Maloney said.

"Sorry," answered Ernest. "I was trying to recall whether or not our parish records would have any information." Now that he did try, he was sure that they wouldn't have. "She never mentioned the matter to me; but it's hard to imagine why her husband would say it if it weren't so."

"I see. And there's no doubt about the gravity of the case? I ordinarily have to require a card from a physician, you know."

Since, last night, Ernest, too, had been disinclined to go to much trouble merely on hearsay, it was not very reasonable to find fault with Father Maloney's attitude. Ernest contented himself with answering: "There's no doubt whatsoever about it. In fact, if you wish to try to confess her, or even to administer viaticum, it is urgent. She may very soon lapse into a coma."

"Well, Mr. Cudlipp, I'm afraid I can't possibly get there for at least an hour or two."

In Heaven there might be more joy over one sinner—or even one careless apostate, one merely material heretic—that repenteth; but on earth the ninety and nine just persons had their rights. And why not? Rome, after waiting on Mrs. Hawley's inclination for twenty or thirty years, might fairly require her to wait an hour.

"But not if I can help it," reflected Ernest. He looked at the ceiling. "I don't think it can wait," he said. "I'll telephone the Dominican Fathers, up here. I daresay they'll find someone free, who can come more quickly."

As he had expected, that didn't go down very well.

Father Maloney said coldly, with restrained exasperation, "It wouldn't be suitable, Mr. Cudlipp. Not at all. I think you would be taking a great deal on yourself."

"Father Maloney," Ernest said, "my only interest in this matter is to provide a very sick woman with what spiritual comfort she seems to require before it's too late. That's all I'm taking on myself. Now, if I'm not to look for it somewhere else, I must rely on you to come immediately. You will? Good." He supplied the address. "It will be a great kindness on your part," he said; but Father Maloney hung up without comment, undoubtedly too angry to trust himself to speak.

"And if I only wouldn't trust myself to speak when someone displeased me," thought Ernest, "I would be a more edifying spectacle. As it is, I let that common little Mick show to advantage beside me—"

Diagonally through the parlor door he had a glimpse of his somber, dark, round face, his eyes snapping, in a big oval mirror— "I must hope it's just my stomach, not my soul," he said. But he felt very well. He felt that alert exhilaration always provoked in him by difficulty or opposition. He might as well have a few words with Mr. Hawley, so he went into the parlor to have them.

Mr. Hawley looked at him with uncertain resentment, or querulousness. Heat and whiskey had dewed his face with sweat. "Now, see here, Mr. Cudlipp," he began loudly, "you got no right to do that without consulting me—"

Noticing Ernest's expression, he moderated his voice for a moment. "We don't hold that. Neither does Mary. We married Episcopalian right here in the Chapel. Her people, they were Catholics, but she couldn't help that—" His voice recovered, though he did not risk looking at Ernest. In that last shot of rye, now that he felt it, he found the spirit of his Orangemen fathers, the musketry at the

Boyne, the Peep-o'-Day Boys, the barnsides over the Ulster border lettered to face the railroad: *God Roast the Pope in Hell!*

"And no-good bums they were!" he said. "My old father knew what to do with sneaking Fenians. And so do I! Mary wants no dirty papist priest—"

"You'd think twice before you said much of that in this saloon you're visiting," Ernest told him. "But, even so, don't bring talk like that home with you. The only place for it's with some other stupid sots at a bar. Sit down and be quiet! Father Maloney will be here presently. Can you treat him with respect, or shall I get a policeman and have you run in for disorderly conduct? You're no help to Mary in this condition, and you're a disgrace to yourself. A Catholic would at least wait until his wife was in her coffin to do his drinking."

Mr. Hawley, confused by the attack, gaped at Ernest. For a moment he stood angry, like a gross, flushed, befuddled baby. He muttered threateningly; yet his heart was not in it. The confidence from the alcohol he had desperately guzzled fell. He hiccoughed, and Ernest could almost see the glow in his stomach turn to a cold sour slop. Terror and loneliness reappeared, unveiled again, just where they were before, ready to face him down; and he could not be comforted. Ernest didn't suppose that Mr. Hawley saw it for what it was, but at least Mr. Hawley could know with certainty that if he lost Mary, he lost something he could not do without. He loved her not in the pride of possession, not in passion, not even in the contentment of affection, but all-pervasively, he loved her as himself. With a completeness and literalness not even to be imagined when, practical strangers, they attempted to symbolize it in the marriage bed, they were indeed made one flesh in the terrible strength of habit. They were one in the ultimate human emotion, perhaps the only emotion vital and enduring—the bond of custom and long use.

Looking at him, Ernest could see Mr. Hawley standing distracted while he met the dreadful, unanswerable question. What could he do without her? What was there to do? Ernest was reasonably sure that, like any man, Mr. Hawley must have fretted a hundred times against the circumstance, thought of other ways to spend his life, other women he would like to have; yet, whether he knew it or not, these things, too, he owed to Mary. Her presence surrounded him with the strong ties to fret against. She and her children gave his life the stability which put glamor in the thought of change. Mary's familiarity was all that created any illusion of novelty in whatever other women he might occasionally fancy. Without Mary, the end came. His existence had no reason; he simply stood at loss and saw the abomination of desolation fallen on him. It would be simpler to telephone the children. Some of them could probably come.

"Sit down," Ernest said, his voice kinder.

He went to the door of the front room to speak to Mr. Johnston about the telephoning. He came back, paying no attention to Mr. Hawley, and went downstairs.

Out on the street, Ernest passed slowly back along the block. At the corner, where he turned to go up to the Chapel House, he paused a moment.

As he had foreseen, Mr. Hawley was coming heavily and cautiously out past the vegetable stands. He did not look around or raise his head. He lumbered straight for the sign hung out above the bar a dozen doors down.

———— • ————

As Ernest climbed the Chapel House stairs he could see someone sitting in the swivel chair before his desk in the

134

office. From a dark silhouette against the bright north light of the window, it resolved itself, as he reached the door, into Lee Breen. Lee was clad in yellow raw silk with a pale blue scarf to match his eyes. Bill Jennings looked at him doubtfully, for Lee had the somewhat irritating habit of frankly examining any of other people's papers and letters which lay to hand. At the moment he was reading the page proof of the year book.

Hearing Ernest's steps, he cocked his wavy blond head, looked up sidelong, pursing his lips. "Hallo!" he said. "What a lot of money you have! Why, I'm enthralled! Why, do you know, it takes thirty pages just to list it. Stocks, bonds, real estate purchases—" He peered at the page. " 'Other real estate is not held at book value—as a memorandum only.' Now, what does that mean? And, look here, is this really your income? Oh, there are offerings, too. And operating receipts! My, my! But I don't think I understand this—" He turned back several pages. " 'Principal Funds and Balance for Investment.' Why the balance?"

"The Senior Warden, who is Mr. Hurst, the banker, evidently did not find all he wanted in the way of sound investments. I haven't examined it."

"Mr. Hurst? You mean, *the* Mr. Hurst? What a catch he must have been! Well, you ought to examine it! Why, do you know you have more than—" he turned the pages quickly looking for the figures "—more than two million dollars in endowments and so on? Imagine! Why, this Holy Innocents' must be the most disgustingly rich church in town. I never realized that before."

Those were the totals that always embarrassed Wilber. Of course, Wilber could reflect that Our Lord's promise had been that if the Kingdom of God and His Righteousness were sought first, all these things would be added.

135

The only question was whether Mr. Hurst and the rich reverent men who for two generations before him had turned their astuteness to the keeping of the parish hadn't been a little officious in seeing that Our Lord fulfilled the engagement so abundantly—whether, in short, your Heavenly Father knoweth you have need of a couple of million dollars.

Ernest said, "Grace and Saint Thomas's have more. Trinity, of course, has ten times as much."

"You don't say!"

Lee faced about, rested his chin on the top of a Malacca stick balanced between his legs. "Well, you know, I think I'm going to Rome—I mean, the Church."

"Alice told me."

"Well, she doesn't know, really. I've had quite a profound religious experience since I saw you last, Ernest. I almost wrote you about it. I didn't, because I had a hunch that the answer really lay in the Catholic Church, not in something like this—" He rapped the open pages of the year book. "This is all too—well, Episcopalian, don't you think? It's not the real thing, I mean. Don't you feel that?"

"No, I don't feel that."

"Well"—Lee swung the stick—"if there's anything in it, I can't see how it can be anywhere except in the Catholic Church. I mean, if you make an act of faith, you shouldn't make it with a lot of reservations, should you? The trouble is, so few people really understand the Catholic Church. I know what you probably think. I know what I used to think myself—"

Exasperated, Ernest said: "You haven't the faintest idea of what I probably think. I doubt if you even have a clear idea of what you used to think yourself; or of what you think now; or of what you will be thinking next month."

"Oh, yes, I have, Ernest," Lee said serenely. "I was very

ill in Germany. I thought I was going to die, and I saw things quite differently. I saw that I had mistaken worldly success for happiness. I saw that my life had no real spiritual direction. I just lived from day to day, you know. Without moral purpose. While I was ill, I think I was passing through what's called the Dark Night of the Senses."

Ernest had to laugh. "Now, surely, Vincent McNamara didn't tell you that?"

"No, but I read about it in a book he let me have. I don't remember what it was called. It had a lot of selections from the lives of different saints, or their writings— Oh, do you know him?"

"Yes, I know him. And I wouldn't tell him that you've passed through the Dark Night of the Senses. What you mean and what Saint-John-of-the-Cross meant aren't the same. Vincent won't think highly of your intelligence if you let him see that you suppose they are."

"Well, now, Ernest, you don't know what I went through. I may be just as able to undergo a mystical experience as you are."

"You may be much more able to. But the state described by that phrase isn't associated with acid indigestion brought on by drinking too much hock. It's a term from the mystical jargon to describe difficulties experienced by those completing the purgative way. They are in transition from meditation to contemplation. It isn't a position you're likely ever to find yourself in. You have to begin by learning to meditate the four last things, and work yourself up. Ask Vincent to give you something on one of the methods. It would bore you so profoundly that you'd soon see the contemplative life isn't for you."

Lee stirred, restless. "Well, that's aside from the point. At any rate, I did have a definite spiritual experience. An awakening. And what I mean is, do you think I ought to join the Catholic Church? Do you think I'd be happier? Father McNamara thinks I would."

Whether you took Lee seriously or not, this indecent anxiety about his happiness was hard to stomach. You could hardly help thinking that Lee greatly exaggerated its importance to the world at large. Ernest felt like assuring him that it really didn't matter much whether he was happy or not. "Father McNamara hasn't known you very long," Ernest said. "So he may be mistaken. I don't think you'd be happier."

"Well, it's hard to tell," Lee said. He looked at Ernest, perplexed, for certainly Lee didn't mean to go to a lot of useless trouble. "But there is a certainty about it, Ernest. Sometimes I feel that all my life I've really been coming to it. Nothing else would do for me—you know: 'Naught shelters thee, who does not shelter Me.'"

Ernest said disagreeably, "The line is, 'who wilt not shelter Me.' Quite possibly you'll find that to be the case. But don't confuse good verse with good sense. They often have nothing in common. I'm suspicious of Vincent's converts. He makes it too much of an emotional matter between him and them."

"Well, look," Lee said. "Why wouldn't you talk to him about it? If you don't think I ought to, you could—"

"Don't be absurd!" said Ernest. "What's there to talk about? If he wants to take you on, that's his business, not mine. I don't think he will. There are many things about Rome I don't like, but one thing everyone must admire is their marvelous common sense—"

"Of course if you feel that way," Lee said. "I don't think it's much to ask. I'd do it for you. You'd know what to ask him; and, between you, you could probably come to some agreement about it. But don't, if you don't want to."

He turned over some letters on the desk. "I was sorry to

have to go out last night," he said. "You aren't offended, are you? I warned you that if Meyer called up, I'd have to. We're supposed to go on the road next week, you know. What became of Alice?"

"Some friend of hers, a woman who is a doctor, put her up."

"Oh! Harriet Stevens. I've always suspected she was a Lesbian, you know. Most amazing creature. She has a mustache. I believe she performs exquisite abortions for the smart set. Such appropriate work. Is Alice taking up with her?"

"You can ask Alice. I expect her to call presently."

"Excuse me! But if I don't mind, you shouldn't, should you? Or is it you she's taking up with? Of course, she always has had a consuming case on you. Well, go ahead, if you want. What's mine is yours."

"Oh, shut up, Lee. You make me sick."

"Oh, no, I don't," said Lee. "You're very fond of me and you know it. Come on. Leave this dreary hole and let's get luncheon. I'm frightfully in need of a drink."

"Then go and get it. I have a luncheon engagement. And a great deal to do, meanwhile. You can come to dinner at the Vicarage tomorrow, if you like."

"I believe I'd better wait and talk to Alice."

"I'll tell her to call you—"

The telephone rang and Lee took possession of it. "That's probably she now," he observed. He tilted back in the chair. "Listen, my good girl," he said, "just where in hell have you been?"

"What?" He made a face. "My error, sir. You're the wrong person. Ernest, it's someone else." He hung up. "Oh, too bad," he said, realizing it. "Embarrassment overcame me. Well, he'll probably call back if he really wants anything."

In fact, the telephone immediately rang again.

Bill Jennings reached over and snatched it, looking as if he would like to sock Lee in the jaw. "It's Mr. Quinn," he told Ernest.

Wilber said, rather breathless, "You haven't seen Mrs. Merrick, have you, sir?"

"No. Didn't she go to New Jersey?"

"Well, you see, last night I offered to take her over. I happened to be going myself, anyway. Mrs. Stone didn't really seem equal to it, and I thought I'd spare her the trouble. So I came around this morning, and we went down—"

"And she gave you the slip," said Ernest. "How?"

"Well, it was simple enough. She said she wanted to go to the ladies' room, here in the ferry house. We're on the Jersey side. And she didn't come out. I waited about half an hour, and then I thought something must have happened to her—she might be ill, or something. Then I wondered if she had managed to take a boat back or— Oh! Good Lord! Wait—"

The receiver was dropped clattering, there was a crash of the booth door opened, a sound of running, some indistinct shouting noises, and complete silence. An operator cut in, saying, "Hello, hello—"

"Keep this connection!" said Ernest. "Reverse the charges, if you want—" But the connection was already broken.

"Who went to New Jersey? Who gave who the slip?" asked Lee. "Why, you look positively pop-eyed, Ernest. Something wrong?"

"Very likely," Ernest said. "Would you mind getting out, Lee?"

"If you insist," Lee said, yawning. "You're like a bear this morning; though, presumably, I'm the one with the head. Meyer lured me into excess. Well, tell Alice to ring me up at the hotel, if she has nothing better to do, will you? I'll doubtless be in the bar. I'll call you after I talk to her about dinner tomorrow, may I?"

He drew on a pair of lemon-colored silk gloves, clapped a tan leghorn hat on his head. "Arrivederci!" he said, poked Ernest lightly in the stomach with his stick, and strolled out.

Ernest put the telephone on the desk. If only Wilber hadn't felt obliged to be so helpful! But, of course, Wilber's perpetual willingness to help was his chief virtue. He was his brother's kindest and most persistent keeper. Wilber would be ashamed of the selfishness which had time to mind only its own business.

Ernest shook his head. "Proffered services," he remembered an old aunt of his remarking cryptically, "stink." If Edna had been obliged to put Lulu on the train herself, the described stratagem couldn't have availed. Everything would have been settled—or, perhaps, he thought prayerfully, it was all right anyway. Wilber's promptness and energy, at least, always could be depended on. And if his breaking-off meant, as very likely it did, that he had caught a glimpse of Lulu, she would have trouble escaping him a second time. At least, Ernest hoped she would. Gazing out at the dull conical curve of slate roof, burning hot in the sun, which covered the apse of the Chapel, he was exhausted by the mere idea of coping with Lulu again today.

Bill said, "I was going to tell you, Mr. Cudlipp, Mr. Wade called up while you were out. He said something about being away for a few days. He said he tried to get you last night. He gave me a telephone number—" Bill turned over the papers until he found it. "I think it's on Long Island, somewhere. Do you want I should call him?"

"No," said Ernest. "Did you get the money?"

Bill worked it out of his pocket and gave it to him. The telephone rang and Ernest lifted the receiver in his other hand.

"Ernie."

"Oh!" said Ernest. "What about it?"

"It's all over. Everything's fine. Here's the address of this place. She's here under her own name—Perkins—did you know? And her sister's address, if you want it." Ernest pulled over a pad and wrote them down. He said: "She's all right?"

"Perfectly, darling. No trouble at all. Oh, dear! She was so frightened, and so afraid I'd know she was. She's really sweet. But such a child! How she can have had two children—"

"I'm very grateful to you."

"I didn't do anything. I just tagged along and held her hand. Oh, she told me you said you'd come and see her this afternoon. I think you ought to. She'll sleep it off and be all right by five o'clock, or so."

"I will."

"So what about lunch, darling?"

"I had to make an engagement. Lee stopped by a few minutes ago. He wants you to call him at the hotel. You'd better eat with him."

"Ernie, how tiresome of you! I don't want to see Lee. I told you I wanted to see you first."

"If you seriously do, come here, at once. I'll have a few minutes before luncheon."

Footsteps had been ascending the stairs and Ernest glanced that way. Astonished, he saw the rector. "'Good morning, Doctor," he said, arising. "Come in. I'll only be a moment."

Alice said: "All right. It will take more than a few minutes."

"My dear, Doctor Lamb is here. I'll have to ring off."

"All right. I'll be along."

Doctor Lamb was still standing.

"Cudlipp," he said, "may I see you alone?"

"Of course," Ernest answered. "Bill, it's almost twelve. The rest of that will keep till Monday. On your way home, will you stop at that florist shop—you know the one." He ripped the sheet from the pad in front of him and copied the address. "Tell them to send some roses up there, will you?"

Doctor Lamb still stood waiting. While Bill covered his typewriter and took his coat, Ernest held up the page proof. "I think this will be very handsome," he said. "Isn't that a fine engraving of the first church! Where did it come from?"

"Why, Mr. Hurst's librarian chanced on it in a completely forgotten portfolio of old Mr. Hurst's. It's an interesting story—" His gaze wandered to Bill, who took hastily the sheet of paper with the address, muttered, abashed, some sort of farewell, and went banging downstairs.

"—quite an interesting story," Doctor Lamb said. He turned and closed the door. "Of course, this is about Father Willever. I felt obliged to see you personally." He stood straight and quiet, his frosty blue gaze fixed on Ernest, his voice dry and distressed. "You know, last night, I was disturbed. I've been on certain convention committees with Father Willever. I've had a number of conversations with him. It seemed to me a great pity if a man of his caliber should be lost to us—well! I thought I'd make some inquiries. I thought there might be some way of approaching him." A slight grimace of revulsion twitched his face. "Of course, I have my information in confidence, and I must respect that; but the source is unimpeachable. Cudlipp, it distresses me very much to have to tell you this;

but you'll see that I have no choice. It's a most degrading and repellent matter. I would really give a great deal not to have known about it." He looked sharply at Ernest and Ernest stood silent, looking back.

"Well," Doctor Lamb said, though not with perfect assurance, "I'm glad to see you didn't know, my dear fellow. I suppose that, quite naturally, he is concealing the truth."

"I know it," said Ernest.

Doctor Lamb's finely molded face took a tinge of color, like a touch of fever. "But, Cudlipp," he said, almost agitated, "if you knew, how could you have him here? The Vicarage is the property of the parish. When you put him up, you involved the parish as well as yourself. You couldn't have thought about it very carefully."

"I didn't expect the parish to be involved. Prudently handled, the matter needn't ever become public knowledge. I have people coming and going all the time. I can't see the remotest chance of anyone feeling curious about him."

"Cudlipp, you surprise me!" Doctor Lamb's expression showed a genuine, fastidious surprise. "That's as good as saying that we may do what we like so long as no one sees us. I'm sure that can't be what you really think."

Ernest said, "What I really think is that Father Willever's position is difficult. I see nothing contrary to faith or morals in offering him a chance to get his emotional balance and decide quietly what he ought to do."

"Faith or morals?" said Doctor Lamb. "Of course there's nothing contrary to them in your act itself. There is nothing contrary to faith or morals—if you must put it so disingenuously, my dear fellow—in giving alms to the poor. But if you give the poor what isn't yours to give, does your charity excuse your stealing? You upset me very much when you take such an attitude."

"I'm sorry," Ernest said. "But I still think there is a legitimate difference between discretion and hypocrisy. I think, if it seems expedient, you may conceal a proper action. I think the obligation to charity is greater than any obligation to convention, or public opinion."

"Cudlipp, you answer me most unfairly. I think I appreciate the right use of discretion. I hope I am a charitable man. I'm sure I'm not perfect either in discretion or charity. Granted. I—"

"I didn't mean that, Doctor Lamb. I meant that in this matter I was taking only the attitude that my conscience recommended to me. If I understand her teaching at all, I think it is the attitude of the Church. Certainly I don't believe that any human act so far separates a man from the Church that it becomes right or necessary for a priest to wash his hands of the matter. That a sinful man ceases to be a Christian may be part of certain Protestant teaching. I don't think it has ever been part of ours—" Ernest checked himself.

"Cudlipp," said Doctor Lamb—his composure and restraint could be called exquisite—"I accept that as an expression of your honest conviction. On most points I am in agreement with it. Father Willever is entitled to all charity and consideration. I don't believe that the Church should repudiate him. The Church is indefectible. Nor that her ministers could, without themselves committing a grave sin, refuse to hear or help him. No. What I have been trying to say is simply that neither he nor anyone else is entitled to anything which is given him at the expense of your good name and reputation. The parish you serve has first claim on both. You have no right to risk your reputation. Your position makes it an integral part of the parish's, the whole Church's reputation."

"I see no reason for any reputation to suffer. I see no possibility of—"

"Cudlipp, how can you tell me that? You're a man of

the world. You are perfectly aware that in this particular matter the possibility is obvious and acute. Nothing is more dangerous and evil! Nothing more insidious! Nothing so poisonously, with so little regard for justice or fact, insinuates itself into a priest's reputation. Think of cases you have known! My dear fellow, are you aware that when I was considering your appointment here such a rumor about you was mentioned to me? It was hinted that you were unduly interested in young men. If it became known later that you had anything to do with Father Willever— No, no!"

"I see," said Ernest. "But apparently you didn't regard the rumor. Why should any intelligent man?"

"I think it would be a waste of time to discuss that, Cudlipp. You oblige me to put the matter in another form. Help Father Willever in any other way you can; but you must not and may not have him in your house."

"I see," repeated Ernest. "Doctor Lamb, I don't like that 'must not' and 'may not.' "

"Cudlipp," said Doctor Lamb, abruptly icy, "do you mean to be impertinent? You don't like it? I'm not asking whether you like it or not! It would appear to be high time for you to realize that you aren't free to consult only your likes and dislikes. I have been advised before this to make that clear to you. I must endeavor to do it. You will have to make up your mind whether your ministry is to act as my Vicar; or whether you feel that you have an independent mission to help such people as Father Willever. Whether the Chapel work is to be your first concern, or whether your many friends—"

The telephone rang.

"There—" said Doctor Lamb. "Answer it. I'll say no more. I think we're both angry. Only this. I'll have to ask you to let me hear from you before night. Come and see me, if you can." He swung the door open and walked to the stairs.

Ernest lifted the telephone. His hand shook a little and blood drummed angrily in his ears. For a moment it muffled the voice at the other end. "Yes, yes," he said. "Oh, John."

"I've been trying to get you. Did you want to see me, sir?"

"Yes. Where are you?"

"Out on Long Island."

"Where? And what are you doing?"

"I'm staying with a friend. I'll be in Monday."

"I want you to come in now."

"Well, I can't, Ernie. I'm busy. Tell me what you want."

Ernest sat down in the swivel chair. "For one thing, I happened to see you at Joseph's last night. I don't want you to go around getting tight in places where I'm known. Especially when you put the bill on my account."

"No one was tight, Ernie. And I'll pay you back as soon as I get my publisher's statements."

"Where were you last night?"

"Oh, I drove out here. Why?"

"Who was the young woman with you?"

"Oh, she's from my publisher's. I had to settle some stuff about a contract."

"Haven't you finished it yet?"

"No, Ernie. As a matter of fact, I haven't. There were a lot of things I had to—"

"John," said Ernest, "John! You aren't thinking quickly this morning. What is it, a couple of eye-openers you've just had?"

"What do you mean?"

"This contract story."

"Do you think she isn't from my publisher? You can call them up and ask them, if you want. She has charge of their publicity department. Her name's Alix—"

"I don't care where she's from. I don't want to know her name. I don't want to know anything about her. I want you to tell her that you've been called back to town and have to leave at once."

"Don't be silly, Ernie. I can't do that."

Ernest waited a moment. Up the steel stairs he could hear the steady, gritty scrape of a practiced step. In the gloom of the hall, Joe's gaunt figure and pale face with its mournful mustaches appeared.

"You can," he said to John. "You're already involved in enough of this."

"I don't know what you're talking about."

Joe reached the door and Ernest shook his head. "I can't see you now," he said. "This afternoon, maybe—"

"Lady downstairs asking for you," Joe said.

"Just a moment, John. What lady?"

"I don't know, Mr. Cudlipp."

"Oh." He had forgotten about Alice. "All right. I'll be down." Joe pivoted in the shadow. The measured gritty scrape began to descend. "John?"

"Yes, sir."

"You know very well what I'm talking about. You know exactly how you're involved, and why. I won't have you starting any new affair. Now, hang up, or you won't be able to pay what you owe on your hostess' telephone bill. And come to town. I'll meet you for dinner and we can talk about what we're going to do."

"It's too absurd, Ernie. I'm not going to do it. I don't know what you're thinking, but I can assure you—"

"No, you can't," said Ernest. "Not any more. John, if you won't do as I say, I'm not going to have you in the Vic-

148

arage. You can't stay with me and go on this way. Do you want me to send your things out there?"

"Oh," said John, "so that's it, is it?"

"That is. Are you coming in?"

"Certainly not. I'll get my things Monday."

"John, why do you make such a fool of yourself?"

"What's it to you?" John said. He hung up.

Ernest dropped the telephone on the desk. He sat a moment looking at it. He got up then, walked over to the open windows and shouted across to the Vicarage: "Lily!"

After a while she appeared, blinking, in the kitchen door. She came out into the sun, moved half way down the yard, and stopped resolutely, lifting a skinny hand to shield her eyes.

He said: "I want you to get lunch for Mr. Willever. Go to the store and get something and fix it for him. Tell him I was called away for a while."

"I got no money to buy anything."

"Well, charge it. I can't spare any now."

"You told me not charge anything at—"

"Hurry. Don't argue."

Downstairs at the front of the lower hall, the big arcuated doors stood open on the blazing steps and street. Sunlight, almost perpendicular, laid a brilliant hot bar on a few inches of the stone threshold. This strip of sunlight threw back a dusky radiance into the vaulted darkness and Ernest could see Alice sitting with patient composure on an oak settee, its high back decorated with cinquefoils, its apex carved into a hideous agnus dei.

She wore black suède sandals, one quietly crossed on the other, just showing under the full hem of a dress of some black stuff covered with a small, neat, white design. Beneath the enormous black brim of her hat, her face was distinct in the reflected light. Her arms were bare, from the puffs at her shoulders to the white gloves crushed down about her wrists.

"Oh, dear!" she said. "Does it look as funny as that? It's really all right, Ernie. I didn't have any clothes at Harriet's, so I had to telephone a shop and buy something they thought would do, without seeing it. You'll get used to it. Or is there something indecent about it I can't see? I was just coming in when your rector went out. I thought I'd made rather a hit with him last night; but he gave me one look, said good morning, put his hat on again and marched off down the street as fast as he could march. It certainly isn't too low in front, and I have a brassière on—"

"Come," said Ernest. "Are you ready for lunch? We'll have it."

"I thought you had a date."

"I did have. I didn't feel up to it at the moment. Do you mind?"

"Why, darling, what's wrong?"

"Nothing in particular. I've had a difficult morning. We'll go to Joseph's. I think we can get there quicker by walking." She stood up and came out onto the hot steps with him.

"Did you have a row with Doctor Lamb?" she asked.

"Does he look to you like the sort of person who would have rows?"

"No, but you do, darling. It comes from being so opinionated, I expect. What did Lee want?"

"I haven't the faintest idea. He discussed religion mainly. That's the precinct police station. I ought to stop in there and see about a vicious little brat who's the brother of a boy who works as my secretary. I'm not going to. Yet perhaps I'd do it, if I weren't so busy with matters not connected with the Chapel."

"Such as taking me to luncheon?"

"I'm entitled to lunch."

She took his arm. "So you did have a row?"

"A difference of opinion only. I think the rector is a little fed up with me. I'm a little fed up with myself. I had to tell John Wade that I was through with him—which irritated me. Wilber was taking Lulu to New Jersey. She got away from him. I suppose she's going to turn up—"

"Well, it's true," said Alice. "You just let them impose on you."

"No, I don't. I get rid of them ruthlessly. You'd be astonished at the number of people I've felt obliged to let out, or, down, in my time. I expect I'll let another one down this afternoon. Either that, or resign."

"Oh, Ernie, I don't think you'd better resign."

"Don't you? I don't think I'd better, either. It would inconvenience me a great deal. Nowadays, I'm ready to temper my independence with consideration, deny myself the satisfaction of cutting a figure, and obey. But it's still up to me to decide whether any particular obedience is sinful, whether it would greatly harm a person I ought to help."

"What person, and what harm?"

"If I were to tell you, I really would be harming him."

"Ernie!"

"Thy friend hath a friend. Thy friend's friend hath—" Jerking it, she freed her hand from his arm, turned her head aside. "Good Lord!" he said.

She drew a breath. "I'm sorry. I'm not at my best this morning. What did you say that for? Ernie, don't you know that if there's anyone in the world you can trust, it's—"

"It's you." Ernest took her arm. "I'd trust you with more than a secret. I'd trust you not to try to learn it, which is a hard thing."

The brim of her hat turned enough so he could see her face again. Her faint smile was composed; but she only said, "I know, Ernie. You've let me out twenty times. And I never stay out. What a bore! I'm just feeling sorry for myself. It seems to me that I've had a long hard life, and where did it get me?"

"What is it about Lee?"

"If I ever get out of this insufferable sun, I'll tell you."

Ernest nodded toward the sign and the two tubbed box bushes up the street in front of Joseph's. "Only that much farther."

He spoke with little enthusiasm, for he felt little, weary with a foreknowledge of the complaint about Lee, and the uselessness of it; since getting rid of Lee was incidental and she would only do it as an act of hope. "Good Lord," he thought, "why should she want me! A middle-aged little runt of an unsuccessful clergyman with a trying disposition, no money, no future; and—the insult on the injury —no chance of being caught, which she knows perfectly well." But of course Alice did not see the facts and who could tell what she did see? Ah, these romanticists! He shook his head.

In the shadow of the door an idle shabby waiter bowed to them. Joseph's great oval face, shining in a creeping sweat, came up the dark passage behind. He elbowed the waiter aside, beaming. "Ah, Mr. Cudlipp!" he panted. "Ah, Madame! I think it is too hot now upstairs. It is better in the garden."

If the consciousness of the seventy dollars Ernest owed him was anywhere there, Joseph concealed it. "But in point of fact," Ernest thought, "I needn't debate about Carl and Doctor Lamb. I couldn't possibly resign. I owe too much money. I certainly can't invite Joseph and how many others to join me in a gesture for my conscience' sake."

The awning was rolled down on the frame of piping over the garden and the resulting shadow was sultry. He saw Alice seated while he stood absent-mindedly, wishing he were somewhere else.

"Do sit down, darling," Alice said. "You make it hotter. I'll have a drink." She removed her gloves. "I can't help it," she said. "I'm going to take this hat off."

It left a straight livid mark high on one side of her forehead. She tossed the hat on the third chair and put a hand to the mark. From her bag she brought out a mirror, looked at herself sadly. Above her ears, curls of the bright reddish hair were darkened, sleek with sweat. "How hateful!" she said. "I can't stay in town any longer while it's like this. I have to be handled with care. Get me a Manhattan, Joseph."

"You don't like whiskey," said Ernest. "Get us both some dry vermouth and ice and Seltzer." He sat down.

Looking in the mirror still, she touched her hair behind, shook her head a little and said, "You don't want me to stay in town, do you?"

"Where are you going?"

She shrugged. "I haven't got that far. Anywhere where it's cool, and I don't have to see Lee. Where can you go when you're thirty-six years old and look like that?"

"It's a question," said Ernest. "I think you're very beautiful, my dear. But I wouldn't reassure you about going anywhere. In the sense you mean, there isn't anywhere."

"Ernie, I'm desperately unhappy. I can't go on with Lee. Why should I? I've spent ten years seeing that everything suited Lee. Why shouldn't something suit me for a change? Except when we're in bed, Lee doesn't give a damn about me. Why should I hang around until I'm so old he won't even give a damn about me then?"

Ernest said, "The purpose of marriage is the propagation of children and the subsequent rearing of them in a Christian home. When that isn't the result, it has no purpose. Having no purpose is likely to become irksome and futile. I see no reason why you should continue to live with Lee, if you don't want to live with him. But you'd miss him. You've lived with him for ten years and you're bound to miss him; just as a person—in your position at least—wouldn't continue, for ten years, anything that was really insufferable. Consequently I don't think there's any sense in divorcing him." He filled the glass of vermouth and broken ice with soda and pushed it over to her. "That's all I have to say, my dear. I can't give you advice of any value or interest to you because we don't regard the same things as valuable or interesting."

"How do you know we don't?" She looked intently at him. Looking back, he could recognize, with a painful, reluctant pity (painful, since he did not believe it could ever be appeased; reluctant, since pity was a form of disparagement), the uneasiness of loss, the insecurity, the restless resentment of a woman not cherished. Lee's stupidity in failing her couldn't have shown clearer, and he was angry at Lee. It would have been so easy for Lee to keep what he had; and properly kept, she would never look at another man. As the man looked at, he could thank Lee for his predicament. He faced it patiently.

"I know, because you're not a Christian," he said. "Like Lee. Your own feelings seem to you the most important things in the world. Suppose I were to say that it isn't especially desirable for you to be happy—in the sense of having things suit you, instead of spending your life trying to arrange things to suit someone else? You'd think I must be crazy. If I suggested that the reason you find your marriage unhappy—if you really do—is that it never was a marriage, but only a compact for fornication with Lee, you'd think I was either insulting, or benighted, or both." He smiled. "Don't worry. It's mostly the heat. In the fall you'll feel quite cheerful—even about Lee. He's vain. In many ways, he's offensive and silly—but what do you expect from the theater? Unless he has changed more than seems likely, he's often kind and sometimes amusing. No. There's no reason to divorce him. Go away and stay until you miss him. What would you like to eat?"

"Nothing. Ernie, what do I have to do to be what you call a Christian?"

"You don't want to be a Christian. Joseph usually has some very good things in aspic. Let me look at the menu." He reached for it; but, putting her hand down, Alice held it closed in front of her on the table. "No," she said. "I'm serious, Ernie."

"Are you?" he asked. "Well, then, I'll answer you seriously. If you want to know what is required of you, what you must believe and what you must do, go to Father McNamara. Since he's angling for Lee, he would be delighted to have you too. I wouldn't feel competent to receive you, for I would be bound to suspect your motives."

She said, absently, "I might do it if it weren't for Lee. But you couldn't do what Lee was doing—it would just be too absurd. If Lee joined the Church, I don't see how anyone else could do it seriously. I could be an Episcopalian. I would be if you wanted me to. Isn't it your religious duty to want me to?"

Ernest said, "If, perhaps many years from now, anything I ever said or did, anything you remembered about me, persuaded you that I was right, and you had always been wrong, all my religious duty toward you would be done."

"I see," she said. "I wonder what I will remember about you?"

"That I was very tiresome and talked a great deal," he said, not entirely at ease.

"I could wish it would be something like that," she answered. "We might as well eat, if you want to, Ernie."

——— • ———

Coming up the steps of the Vicarage, Ernest could hear the piano in the back room—a few casual bars, a fragment of simple tune soon broken off, listlessly begun again after a moment. In the sound of it could be read Carl Willever's state of mind, distracted and restless. The scattered notes fell in the silence of the empty, shadowed house with melancholy of ennui, of helpless, hopeless inanition. He had nothing to do.

At Holy Trinity, the Fathers would this moment be passing from their short arbitrary recreation period around the cloister in unquestioned habit, filing into their chapel stalls. On the stroke of two o'clock their voices broke out, chanting from side to side: *Haste thee, O God, to deliver me* . . . The ninth hour, the Death on the Cross, was upon them— *Make haste to help me, O Lord.* They had been up since dawn. They felt the fatigue of the morning routine; the noon meal made them torpid.

How vain the effort! How small the accomplishment! How empty the afternoon! *Let them be ashamed and confounded that seek after my soul: let them be turned backwards and put to confusion that wish me evil* . . .

Now the discouraged took heart, the weary were refreshed, the lethargic roused themselves. A tide of plainsong bore them up; familiar words chanted themselves—reassuring, inevitable. Twenty minutes later they were back at their diverse work. The noonday demon had come, found them all busy, and gone.

Ernest walked through the little vestibule.

He stopped, seeing to his right, in the door of the front room, a plain stocky girl in a somewhat soiled white skirt and light blue cotton blouse. A blue béret was pulled down on the side of her head. Ernest did not think he had ever seen her before, but she looked like one of the girls who might be in some Chapel House organization. He said: "How do you do? Can I help you?"

Embarrassed, she answered, "You're Mr. Cudlipp, aren't you? I came up with Wilber. He just went over to the office, or something, looking for you. I'm Peg Schwartz."

Then, of course, she was the girl with the good head who was perfectly able to see that atheism was not an integral part of Communism. Ernest gazed at her with interest. She looked little more than twenty, and her consciously bold, decided air became her; but she was far from easy. It might be because Ernest's reversed collar embarrassed her. If that were the case, what a curious conflict she must be suffering over Wilber. Even if Wilber never let her see him in clerical clothes, he was a minister, and the wincing she must have done—facing Wilber, facing her former friends, facing herself alone—over the intellectual Scandal of the Cross was easy to imagine. Ernest said sympathetically, "Come in. Sit down. I'm glad to see you, Peg. Wilber has spoken of you."

She stepped backward awkwardly and he went into the front room with her. To himself, he said: "But I'd be gladder if she were pretty. What on earth is Wilber up to?" He found a package of cigarettes and held them out to her. "I don't smoke," she said. She was still standing up, her embarrassment so marked and extraordinary that he might as well notice it. "Is something wrong?" he asked.

She answered: "Yes, there is. I guess Wilber'd better tell

you about it. I was just meeting him, you see. I don't really know—"

"Well, perhaps I'd better go over and find him. You sit down, and I will."

He went out. At the end of the hall, he pushed open the partly closed door of the back room. "Carl," he said, "did you get lunch all right?"

Carl turned from the piano. "Yes, I did, thanks," he said. "Are you—"

"I'll be back in a few minutes. I have to see my assistant."

"If you mean that old fellow, he went upstairs a little while ago."

"No, this is a boy from the seminary."

In the shadows, in that shabby suit, Carl sat still on the piano bench, lax, bloated, pasty. He looked like a furtive, obscene old man, "—and I suppose," Ernest thought, his heart sinking, "that's just what he is, by any popular definition. Next time he'll get a jail sentence."

You could see the obscure paragraph in the papers—a former priest—impairing the morals of a minor, probably. For the truth was, such things didn't get better, they got worse. Doctor Lamb was right enough and reasonable enough. You would have to recognize the necessary gap between the practice you were put to and the aspiration which you preached. If what you saw there was Carl Willever, no one but a fool would trust him. You might hope and pray, but you could not expect that anything you did would avail against what you saw. Without the robes of his Order, without what they implied in the security of a living, in the self-respect, and, probably, pride, of a reputation high in its little field, he had nothing left, he stood for nothing, he was nothing. Ernest closed the door and went on downstairs.

In the kitchen Lily was sound asleep, hunched in a rocking chair in the corner. Ernest went through, out into the burning light of the backyard. The wooden gate at the corner swung and Wilber appeared. "Thank God, I've found you, sir," he said. "The most terrible thing—"

"Now, now," said Ernest.

"I don't know what to say! Of course it was my fault. If I hadn't been such a fool—"

Ernest took his arm, turned him about, and went back through the gate with him. In the cool darkness of the basement door of the Chapel House he brought him to a halt. "Now, get hold of yourself," he said.

"I ought never to have— I can see now that what happened was that when I ran after her, she lost her head; or didn't look where she was going—"

"And what happened?"

"Well, this ferryboat was going out. She may have thought she could get on it, though it was past the ends of the pier. Before anyone could stop her, she—er—fell between it and the dock. And—"

"Is she dead?"

"Yes."

"Wilber, you didn't have anything to do with it. That was bound to happen sooner or later."

"If I hadn't run after her, she might not have fallen—"

"She didn't fall. She jumped." Ernest looked at him. "Wilber, Wilber! This isn't any way for you to behave. You aren't a child. It's not your fault. But even if it were, you'd still have to meet it better than that. Come up to the office. I want to talk to you."

"Oh—well, I brought Miss Schwartz up with me. Maybe I—"

"I know. I saw her. She'll wait."

The sun had moved, beginning to fall in the back windows of the Vicar's office. Outside, the curved roof, the thin lancet windows of the Chapel apse were at last shaded. "Sit down," Ernest said. "Where did they take her?"

"The police took her to the morgue. They had a pulmotor squad down and they worked some time. I told them I'd let them know. I couldn't give them any particulars, really. I'm afraid they'll want someone else to identify the body."

"Yes. I'll take care of it. You didn't call up Mrs. Stone, did you?"

"No. I thought I should see you. I called you, but—"

"I was out to lunch."

He could hear Alice saying, "—you just let them impose on you—" and his own response, "Oh, no, I don't. I get rid of them ruthlessly." On the far wall hung a large Church Kalender from a religious publishing house—the months spread out in two-inch numerals. Ernest looked at them wearily—the Gothic shapes, the liturgical colors in pale printing inks. At the top, Saint Peter and Saint John, in the well-known—too well-known—painting pressed with their excess of carefully depicted zeal through the color-process dawn to the empty sepulcher. What pain could he feel except that sentimental pain of finding that he felt none? It was the last inevitable indignity for Lulu —the sodden body fished out of dirty water, the pulmotor mask clamped over the worn, disfigured face; finally, with shrugs, the vain business given up.

Wilber, a nervous, upset stranger, was the only actual mourner; and his mourning could be little more than the shocked, revolted pity of a stranger, who might fear that he would remember as long as he lived a horrible, sad, shabby old woman lying drenched and dead on the ferry-house floor.

Ernest said, "Take your Peg somewhere and entertain her. I like her. But don't marry her if you can help it."

Wilber roused himself, startled. "Well, I—"

"Wilber, if you must marry, marry someone with money. There isn't any reason why the Church should have to support a wife and family for you. As long as you haven't any, you can get along on what would be offered you anywhere. And you don't need a wife, you know. Don't let the Groupers make you think you do."

"What do you mean, sir?"

"Διὰ δὲ τὰς πορνείας—" said Ernest. "Supposing my Greek is still intelligible. It's not the happiest attitude."

Wilber flushed. "You aren't fair to them, if you think they make as simple a matter as just avoiding fornication out of it, sir."

"What they make of it isn't important. You know what you're making of it."

"Well, I don't think she'd have me, anyway. So—"

"Of course she'll have you! Do you imagine that she'd be tagging around with you this way if she wouldn't? You know your Communist friends. What do you think they say to her about it?"

"Well, I don't know. But there's a lot to her, Padre—" He returned Ernest's look, worried, but seriously resolved, and shook his head. "And we can't all be like you, sir."

"What do you think I'm like?" asked Ernest. "Never mind. I'm like a man considerably worse than forty who has been through a lot. I hope you aren't all like me. Now, get along. Buy her a soda and go to the movies. But when you marry, marry somebody who has a lot of money and knows how to pour tea for the Women's Auxiliary."

He stood up. "Wilber," he said, "it was hard on you; but I'm glad you were there this morning. I'm glad to know what really happened. Thank you. And bring your

Peg to supper. There's always a chance I'll think differently if I get to know her."

"Okay, Padre," Wilber said. He had shaken off his consternation of ten minutes ago. Restored now, he was able to indulge the Vicar's crotchets. He knew better than to argue. He knew better than the Vicar. "We'll be there."

Ernest took up a pencil. With the end of it he began slowly, picking out numeral after numeral, to dial Edna Stone's number. He tilted back in the chair. "Edna," he said.

"Oh, Ernie. Did she get off all right?"

"No, she didn't. She got away from Mr. Quinn and jumped off a ferry slip. Do you want to come over and identify her with me this evening?"

"Oh, my God!"

"I don't think you do. There's no reason why you should."

"Ernie, how horrible!"

"Do you think so?"

———— • ————

In the kitchen, Lily, awake and morose, was listlessly turning a dish over and over under a running tap to rinse it. "Mr. Cudlipp, there was a girl upstairs," she announced. "She said she was waiting for Mr. Quinn. I told her Mr. Quinn don't live here. I don't know what she wanted. I don't know whether you want her there or not."

"Didn't Mr. Quinn come for her?"

"I don't know. I went upstairs. When I came down she was gone. I went to pick up Mr. Johnston's room; but he's there lying asleep on his bed. That man I fix lunch for don't eat any of it. I have plenty to do without fixing lunch for people who don't eat it. I—"

"It's too bad about you," Ernest said. "As well as dinner

at noon, we're having supper in, tomorrow; and there'll be people here. Mr. Quinn, and a friend, and probably some other people."

"Mr. Wade going to be here?"

"I don't think so."

"Well, he better stay away. Some man was looking for him this morning to give him a court paper. I said I didn't know anything about it. I didn't know where he was—" She gave Ernest a dour, accusing look, as though she felt that the arrival of a man with a summons for someone in the house was more than anybody could expect her to stand.

"You did quite right," said Ernest. "It isn't any of your business."

"Well, I just said, how could I tell? Mr. Wade comes in all hours of day and night, drinking liquor and—"

"That is none of your business, either. Have what you like for supper tomorrow. But I want it to be a good one."

"It'll be a good enough one, just so I don't have you tell me five, and then I find eight, or who knows what to serve. I have to have some idea. I—"

"You have some idea. Here's money. It's all you can have. Now, go and get your marketing done." As he went upstairs he could hear her reviewing her complaint about John, a mumbling dialogue in which she curtly addressed and sharply answered herself. Ernest shrugged. He was sorry if John was in a jam about money—probably all those monogrammed handkerchiefs, custom-made dress shirts, and pigskin toilet cases had come home to roost— but, then, John might as well be in a jam. Until it was conclusively demonstrated to him that the eventual vexations and annoyances of being unable to pay for them largely spoiled the pleasure of possessing such unnecessarily fine raiment— "Well," he said aloud, "the size of it is, I don't know what to do with him. I couldn't know less if

I were his father. It's time I gave it up, and I ought to be glad that I can give it up."

He ought to be; but he felt instead a frustrated soreness of heart. Perhaps it was like that distracted anger and disappointment which Bill Jennings described in his father. Mr. Jennings, an angry, simple man, taking a strap to the incorrigible Jimmy, would beat him in what was truly and largely a frenzy of love. He would feel, as well as exasperation, a panic of foreboding over what might happen to Jimmy unless Mr. Jennings could hurt and frighten him so much that Jimmy would stay where he was safe and never do that again.

Of course, in Jimmy's case, the failure was lamentable; but that didn't necessarily reflect on the method, and couldn't reflect on the motive. Jimmy wouldn't have been beaten until he clearly needed beating. And why he should need it, why he couldn't be like Bill—furious, his father must have asked him that a hundred times. There was no possible answer. Since it was unanswerable, the folly of Wilber's hopeful notions became apparent. On this trifle—it was Jeremy Taylor's wild, indeterminate, infinite appetite of man—the whole scheme—the appeal to reason, the assumption of good will, the faith in a nobler disinterestedness—by which Wilber and his friends purposed to establish the millennium, collapsed. It would be more of a credit to their intelligence if they purposed, under cover of the talk, nothing but an improvement of their own fortunes; for the new day would still find them being born Jimmy and Bill, and who but a simpleton could suppose that sweet social reasonableness would make Jimmy any less Jimmy—

Ernest stopped at the head of the stairs. The door to the back room was open. Glancing in, Ernest saw that Carl Willever was no longer there. Going on upstairs, he found Mr.

Johnston's door open, too. Mr. Johnston must have heard him, for he called, "Lily, do you want to come in here now? I'll—"

Ernest stepped in. Mr. Johnston had been lying on the bed. Struggling to sit up, he put a hand to his forehead, from which a folded damp cloth fell off. He had removed his shoes and coat, but not his waistcoat or collar. Blinking, he rubbed his sore red eyes and fumbled for his glasses on the bedside table. "Oh, Vicar!" he said. "I had a slight headache. I thought I'd take a moment's rest."

"Lie down," said Ernest. "Take it."

"I must go back and see Mrs. Hawley shortly. I telephoned to her daughter, who finally arrived. By that time Doctor Casali had returned and administered an opiate."

"Did Father Maloney come?"

"Oh, yes. Very promptly. Previous to that. He seemed to have some success with her— I withdrew, of course. At least he appeared satisfied, and I thought she appeared somewhat calmed. I think you were very wise to send for him. At such a moment it would be quite wrong to take a narrow view." He rubbed his forehead. "I don't know what became of Mr. Hawley. I didn't see him again. Perhaps it was just as well. I was a little concerned about Doctor Casali and Father Maloney. You know, the Roman Catholics don't consider it lawful to administer drugs with the intention that the patient shall die without recovering consciousness. I discovered that in the North. I see their point; but in a case like this I find it hard to— Well, naturally, they have every right to their belief. Fortunately Doctor Casali was much delayed. I was afraid he might return while Father Maloney was there and make his intention obvious. Well, I mustn't lie here—"

"I think you should. If the daughter's there, what could you do? I'll come in and wake you in an hour."

165

"Well, perhaps I will. I told Doctor Casali I'd give her another injection; but it wouldn't be quite time yet. I took an aspirin and I think my head will soon be better."

"Good. I'm going to read your sermon. I haven't had a chance to."

In fact, he had left it, forgotten, on his bureau, Ernest remembered now. He drew Mr. Johnston's door closed and went into his bedroom. Slow steps began to descend from the floor above. Ernest took the manuscript and went back into the hall.

"Hello," Carl Willever said. "Your young fellow came back here, I think. I saw him in the hall."

"Yes. I found him. Come on down. It's as cool in the back room as anywhere. I've some free time at last."

They went down in silence. Ernest shut the door after them, pulled off his coat and threw it on a chair. "Carl," he said, "you were right, and I was wrong. I can't keep you here. Someone knows the story—someone Doctor Lamb was able to get at this morning. Who would it be? Not anyone at the monastery—"

"I wouldn't be too sure of that," Carl said. "I could name a couple of old or young bastards."

"Well, I don't think so. Doctor Lamb wouldn't be discussing it over a telephone toll line. I think someone up there must have written someone he knows in town—"

"It doesn't make much difference, does it? Well, you can't say I didn't tell you last night! I thought you were being a little nobler than the law allows."

He had sat down on the bench, his back to the piano, his round shoulders bent forward, his white face sagging with heat and fatigue. He stared at Ernest. His lips began to quiver a little and he said: "So that's that. Well. I'd better not contaminate the place any longer. I'll get along. I suppose you still haven't got a dollar?"

"I'll give you what I have," Ernest said. "Carl, I said I couldn't put you up here. That doesn't mean that I won't help you. Now, let's think it out. If you leave here, what do you think you'll do?"

"What the hell would you expect me to do?" Carl Willever said. "If I'm going to eat, I'd better get a job. You don't need a janitor, do you?"

"Haven't you any relatives?"

"Yes, they'd be glad to see me! They're all good Christians, too. I have about a thousand devoted friends. Every one of them would let out a squeal and run for his life. You ought to know."

"Yes, I should," said Ernest. "But sometimes people will be amazingly kind, amazingly generous, if they possibly can. Wasn't John Benham a friend of yours?"

"How do I know?"

"Come, come," Ernest said. "Don't be such a baby, Carl! He certainly won't do anything for you if he doesn't know that you need anything done. I have to obey my rector. I'm in a subordinate position. He's not. He has a parish in Philadelphia, and I think he'd be able to—"

"That canting little rat! I can just see myself going down and licking his boots for a handout!"

"What do you see yourself doing?"

"I see myself bumming a dollar off you and getting the hell out of here. It would be something to get away from the strong stink of Episcopalianism. You're all such damned hypocrites! There's this to be said for the Roman Church, they aren't so worried about their own respectability that—that—"

"That what?" asked Ernest. He found a cigarette and lit it. "Well, why don't you go there? You might very well find that it was the answer. I don't know by what process of thought or impulse you came to do what you did—"

"Do what I did!" mimicked Carl. "Don't you even know a name for it?" He supplied several. "You don't like them, do you?"

"No, I don't," said Ernest.

"You bet you don't! It's all part of this damned farce you make your living out of. You couldn't any more admit the simple truth about anything— What do you believe, anyway? Do you dare to tell me?"

"You know what I believe. It's what you believe yourself when you quiet down. This is a stupid pose, Carl. If you didn't care, it would never occur to you to get so excited over it. I think you would do very well to apply for reception. Go and see Vincent McNamara. I happen to know he's in town."

"Little Vinny!" snorted Carl. "My God! Is he still running around snapping actresses' garters? That's a hot one! If there ever was a fake, he's it. He's one of those I'll-take-you-home-again-Kathleen Irishmen who knows which side the butter's on. I could tell you plenty about him."

Ernest said, "Nonsense. You know nothing about him, except that you've always wondered if he didn't do the right thing when he left Holy Trinity and went over."

"That's where you're wrong. I never wondered. The only difference is, if you can stand the company, the Roman Church is a better racket for a poor boy. You don't have to be polite to the parishioners. You don't have to account to some vestry for the cash—"

"The Methodist machine is something to ride, too; if you can get high enough in it," Ernest said indulgently. "Why don't you investigate that?"

"I'm still waiting to hear what you believe."

Resigned, Ernest said: "I believe in one catholic and apostolic church—the communion of saints, the forgiveness of sins, the life in the world to come. I know they must be so, just as I know that God sees me, and that my Redeemer liveth. My effort is to see Him. I do. I have seen Him. I don't mean that He is manifest to my senses, or that I see any convincing trace of Him in the firmament. But when my heart is clear enough, I see Him in my heart."

"Oh, oh!" said Carl.

"If you think that's too pretty, I'll say my reins also instruct me in the night seasons. You asked. I've tried to tell you. What more can I say?"

"You could come clean and admit you think it's a lot of bunk."

"You sound like a sophomore," said Ernest. "Good God, can you live forty years and see nothing? Find out nothing about life? Learn nothing about people? My soul doth magnify the Lord! He hath scattered the proud in the imagination of their hearts; He hath put down the mighty from their seat! Any fool has seen it, time after time. No one was prouder than I was twenty years ago—you see me. By your own inordinate act, you're pretty well put down, Carl. Look closely at your fellow men, and you will see in what just and unpredictable ways He fills the hungry with good things."

"Blah!" said Carl. "That's all language."

His sullen, puffy, rather snouty face swung back and forth as he shook his head, uneasy, violent. "It won't do, I tell you. I never believed it. I don't now. I never will. But I know the language. When I want to, I can handle it—" His mouth bent into a momentary contemptuous smile. "Better than you ever could! Hell, you don't know how to preach! You have no feelings. You have no real personality. I knew you never had it in you. At the seminary you impressed a lot of—" He broke off, his plump short hands clenched.

On the clean new back of Holy Innocents' Dispensary

169

one window, high up, without an awning, was catching the afternoon sun in a molten flash, like a mirror. The long shaft of the reflection struck down across the dreary backyards, through the open window, and began to fall on the piano behind Carl. This unexpected light touched him as he rocked back, and, startled, he turned his head.

He stared a moment at the blinding wink of the window, at the pale beams on the piano keys and the dusty wood. Some intolerable sadness in this false sunshine seemed to unnerve him. The blatant, labored cynicism dissolved visibly away in a baffling transformation which was hardly more convincing. Yet the tears coming into his eyes were real. The torment of mind, which made him shake, must be real too. "Good God, Ernest," he said, "what can I do? I can't go on this way. I couldn't get a job. I can't go back—I don't believe anything, I tell you!"

Ernest put a new cigarette in his mouth. "You don't have to believe anything," he said. "All they ask of you is that you should be penitent. It would be hard to doubt that you're that."

Carl Willever's face changed once more. The moist eyes seemed to dry up. "Oh," he said softly, "you think I ought to go back. You think it doesn't matter whether I believe it or not?"

"Under the circumstances, I think it matters very little," Ernest said. "Go back, Carl. You can live there. You're better off there than you would be anywhere else. Call it hypocrisy, if you must. There's a greater sin. It's presumption. I've committed it too many times. I know all about it. I think you would be blamed less for considering what is expedient, than—"

"Ah!" said Carl harshly. His face recovered a kind of firmness. His eyes glittered. "Expediency never faileth!" He gave a short, malicious laugh. "But whether there be prophecies, they shall fail; whether there be tongues, they shall cease; whether there be knowledge, it shall vanish away!" His voice gained strength. "Though I give my body to be burned, and have not expediency—" He got to his feet and came forward.

Ernest sat still, the cigarette smoking quietly in the corner of his mouth.

Carl Willever lowered his chin, thrust his face out. "I never really liked you much before, Ernest," he said, his voice intense, slow and dramatic. "I was never sure I understood you. But now I think we ought to be friends. God, yes! You couldn't despise me any more than I despise you! You've just taught me a lot. You're very kind."

His right hand swept out and, awkwardly, without much force, he struck Ernest across the face. The cigarette flew ten feet and showered sparks on the floor. "That's what I think of you," he whispered. "Whatever my sin, at least I've been honest. No. By Heaven, at last I am honest! You damned hypocrite!"

Ernest's cheek and nose stung slightly from the blow. He stood up; and Carl, interrupted, recoiled a step. "Good Lord!" Ernest said. "Do you think I'm going to hit you back?" He went and trod out the burning cigarette end. "Will five dollars buy your ticket?" He took the bill from his pocketbook.

Carl Willever came forward again. "Oh, yes," he said. "Oh, yes." He laughed, loud and forced. "Buy my ticket?" he said. "Why, you pop-eyed little prig, five dollars buys an immortal soul. I don't have to tell you that. You know that."

Ernest smiled. "Take it," he said. "Take it. I'm glad if you feel better. But don't shout. Mr. Johnston has a headache. He's trying to get a nap."

"Keep your money." Carl's face was colored dark in the

easy excess of his new feelings. "I can get back. I've been a pilgrim in my time. There are roads. Better men than I have walked them. It's not comfortable. Oh, no. It's not expedient! A Pullman seat would suit you better. I want none of your money. I want nothing of yours." Suiting, perhaps a shade too consciously, his action to the violence of his words, he pulled the door open. "When I see the devil," he said, "I know, at least, that I am God's child."

He strode down the hall to the open front door.

Ernest called, "Good-by, Carl! Good luck!"

He got no answer and he sat still a moment, trying to guess what satisfying sight of himself Carl had fixed his mind on now. Probably, as Carl said, it was the pilgrim. Dusty and footsore, he was lifting the great knocker on the gate at Holy Trinity, seeing the astounded face of the lay brother who opened. *Father, I have sinned against heaven, and before thee . . .*

Doubtless Carl saw more than that. His rapid inspiration might compass all the great drama ready and waiting for him—as a recluse, perhaps; his preaching talent put away forever. Perhaps he would never speak a word again. Year after year he might move in portentous silence, not mingling with the community, between his cell and his chapel stall—eyes always on the ground; hands hidden in the sleeves of his cowl; lowered face, overhung by his hood, shown to no one.

Prodigies of fasting, exhausting vigils, perpetual prayer would soon make Father Willever a legend. Assuredly he would be allowed a hair shirt. It might be known that he had appealed (writing on his slate, since he never spoke) to Father Superior for permission to keep a cord discipline; and perhaps he had been granted the Cistercian use, after the night office Fridays— Ernest shook his head; but it wasn't impossible, he knew. Something like that—it would be the real thing, not any pretense; for to believe the part played it was necessary to feel the pains—might satisfy Carl.

If it satisfied him, Carl might very well prove to be, once he had found his formula, among the few chosen from the many, on occasion, called. Surely he had the temperament to support the awful rigors of emotional religion. Ah, yes, yes! Saint James' knees were calloused like a camel's. Peter, Cardinal Damian, used for his food that vessel in which he washed the sores of beggars. Fishes, as though dynamited, rose from the depths at Rimini! Three times Friar Bernard trod with his feet upon his throat and upon his mouth. In fever and sickness, kissing lepers, lifting churches through the air, insensible to fire, walking safely on the sea, falling in fits and raging in tongues—

Ernest thought: "Blessed Carl Willever, O.H.T.!" That amused him. He did not want to think of any other aspect of it at the moment. Sitting down in the chair by the window, he unfolded Mr. Johnston's manuscript.

———— • ————

At the head of the first sheet, Mr. Johnston had written in the loose, impressionistic scrawl of a person who does not see well: *The Fifth Chapter of the Gospel According to Saint Luke; the Sixth Verse. When they had this done, they enclosed a great multitude of fishes; and their net brake.*

Faced with it, Ernest thought: "I can never get through this! Shall I have him read it to me? No, that would be much worse. I'll have to make an effort—"

He read: *Perhaps the greatest significance of this story of the miraculous draught of fishes is to be found in its effect on Simon Peter. Saint Luke tells us that he fell down at Jesus' knees. He cried: Depart from me; for I am*

173

a sinful man, O Lord! At first glance, this is a very— Mr. Johnston had crossed out the word, written in another, and crossed that out, finally scrawled what looked like "cryptic" *—this is a very cryptic thing for him to say. Why did the sense of his sins oppress him so suddenly? The Gospel says that he spoke as he did because he was astonished by the number of fishes.*

This must, indeed, have been an astonishing experience, and one which would compel anyone to take thought! A few fishes might have been expected; although Saint Peter tells Our Lord that they had toiled all night and caught nothing. Still, some fish would probably sooner or later have returned to that part of the lake naturally. But what did they find? A great multitude of fishes! So many, so amazing a number, that they had to beckon to their partners to bring up another boat and help them, for the net broke. That is, it was very likely attached to floats, and when they tried to gather in the floats, there were so many fish inside the net that the float line was not equal to the strain and came loose from the net proper. There were so many fish that, when they had somehow succeeded in hauling them in, both boats began to sink, Saint Luke says. This would assuredly manifest a power which could only be divine—

Ernest fumbled patiently for a cigarette, but there were no more in the package. He shifted in the chair. He thought of Mr. Johnston, his grave worn face, the pen haltingly pursuing his laborious thought. The best explanation would certainly seem to be that the float line came loose from the net proper.

Now it might be wondered why Our Lord would cause so many fishes to be in the net that it would break? Why not only as many as the net could conveniently hold? Then, too, the boats began to sink! The miracle put the

*fishermen in grave danger and Jesus would certainly not
want them to drown. To understand it, we must remember that these men were fishermen. They were experienced with fish and boats. No doubt they could swim. Our
Lord would take all this into consideration when he
wished to display his power in a way that would impress
them. No ordinary draught would do, for they might mistake it for ordinary good luck. It would have to break the
net and cause the boats to sink if they were to understand.
How well the divine plan proved itself when Peter fell at
Jesus' knees. The multitude of fishes had done their work.
Jesus was able to say to him, From henceforth thou shalt
catch men!*

*But to grasp this great lesson in its entirety we must go
back a little. This was not the first time Saint Peter had
met Our Lord. No. His brother Andrew had brought him
to the Saviour by the banks of Jordan—*

"No, no!" thought Ernest. "I wish I could, but I can't.
There's nothing to be done. He will simply have to use it."

Folding the sheets, he sat still a moment, his mind vacant. Aloud, he said: "I doubt if I could have kept Carl
here. We'd have had some sort of scene the first time I
gave him a chance to make it." But he thought a moment
of resigning anyway. "Well, you can't," he said; "you'd be
almost as badly off as Carl. You will have to stick it out."

The last time he had seriously thought of throwing up a
job was at Saint Matthew's, years ago. Though he forgot
exactly what the difference with Doctor Ogilvie had been,
he could remember that the reason he hadn't resigned was
that he didn't think anyone else would be capable of carry-
ing on those Sunday evening "vesper" services. Ernest's sol-
emnly thought-out conclusion came to what he owed the
miscellaneous mob he had attracted. At the time the im-
plication did not impress him—or, at least, did not seem

to him a reflection on his results—but he knew very well that many of those who came would not keep coming if he left. You couldn't say that about the Chapel people. For the majority, attendance was part of an unspoken bargain between them and Holy Innocents'. They would keep coming as long as they were given reason to.

"Ah," Ernest thought, "how tired I am! How tired! Maybe I ought to resign. Maybe somebody who isn't tired —Wilber would do more than I can. They like him. As a matter of fact, Wilber could marry his girl. She'd be perfectly all right here, and so would he—"

But he knew better than that. Doctor Lamb wouldn't even consider Wilber—he was too young. As for Holy Innocents' Vestry, it would take no time at all for Wilber's sociological views to get to them. Ernest could see their faces. Not less than six had various, neat, old-fashioned forms of white mustaches. Two were invariably bundled to their chins with Ascot ties. They were somewhat trembly, but shrewd, kind, rich old men; with a few ventures in young blood of no more than fifty, to show their interest in a different point of view; and one cultivated, intelligent, and affable converted Jew whose name had been changed from Steinthal to Stonington, to show their broad-mindedness.

It wasn't that Communism would alarm them. As a matter of business routine, men like Mr. Hurst were kept better informed of actual conditions than any Communist could be. With a possible timid, retired exception or two, they knew that the revolution was nonsense. It was a moral matter, only. Communism was silly, wrong; an idea which could only be entertained by bad, low, irresponsible people. They certainly would not agree to maintain at Saint Ambrose's Chapel a bad, low, irresponsible Vicar.

If Communism wasn't enough, there was also Wilber's

uncompromising pacifism. Rectors of Holy Innocents' had been, since the days of the Civil War, permanent chaplains of a notable National Guard regiment. Remembering Wilber's amusement last night, Ernest guessed that the letter to the *Churchman* must contain some further observations of Wilber's on abolishing the army and navy chaplaincies. Wilber felt that they represented a wicked aid and comfort to war-makers. As a theological student, working part of his time as an assistant, Wilber could have his notions, and Doctor Lamb could even consider them well-expressed. As the Vicar, they would be a piece of inexcusable impudence. No. It wouldn't do.

Ernest put Mr. Johnston's manuscript in his pocket, went into the hall and up the stairs. He knocked on Mr. Johnston's door.

Mr. Johnston was already up.

"Oh, thank you, Vicar," he said. "I did fall asleep." Stiffly, he moved to the bureau and took a comb which he passed through his mussed gray hair. "If you'll excuse me, I'll wash a little, I think," he said. "I'll only be a moment."

Left alone, Ernest laid the manuscript on the bureau. The room was almost entirely bare. On the small writing-table two framed photographs were propped against the wall behind—Bishop Bentley, the Suffragan of Alaska, standing in his furs with a half dozen harnessed dogs at his feet. The other was an enlarged snapshot. It showed a half circle of Indians or Eskimos gathered before a low frame building surmounted by a cross. In barrenness freezing and terrible, a snow slope spotted with occasional dark masses of rock or boulders swept out and up, forming the whole background. There was a bottle of ink, a few steel pens, some sheets of the Vicarage's printed stationery. On the bureau lay an old Bible in worn faded binding; and on the Bible, a shabby little copy of the *Imitation of Christ*.

Mr. Johnston came into the room. He fitted his glasses on carefully. "I feel much refreshed," he said. He pulled a silver watch from his waistcoat pocket and consulted it. "I think it will be almost time for me to give Mrs. Hawley that other injection." He sat down on the edge of the bed, struggling with a shoe horn to lever his ungainly black-socked feet into his big shoes.

"I've read your sermon—" Ernest nodded toward it on the bureau. "I like it."

"Then you think it will do?" Mr. Johnston peered up at him, gratified. "That takes a great load off my mind! I shall soon get into the way of it, I think. Once started, I found that it came more easily than I expected. I mustn't trouble you about it again. It was very kind of you to look at it."

"It was no trouble," said Ernest.

Mr. Johnston put his coat on. "Doctor Casali told me he would be at the Dispensary; so I planned to stop there to let him know how she is, afterward. But if you should want me for anything, I'd come back here directly. There can be nothing to tell him. We must simply hope that it won't be prolonged."

"I'm going out," Ernest answered. "I'm obliged to go over to New Jersey this evening on a private matter. I won't be here, so I'm sure I won't need you for anything—"

He paused, wishing to add some suggestion, for Mr. Johnston had done enough, surely. To suggest that; to point out that there was no need for him to watch Mrs. Hawley die—or put off dying—would be only to offer him a hot evening alone in the Vicarage.

Yet no idea came to him. Ernest could think of nothing in which Mr. Johnston would plausibly find amusement;

and so he had his answer. Mr. Johnston needed no amusements, no suggestions. The rewards of his hard, bare, devoted life, the unsearchable riches of Christ, were given him in the perfect freedom and perfect joy of needing nothing.

Ernest smiled. He was rebuked out of his own mouth. The hungry were, indeed, filled.

———— • ————

It was a narrow, white-fronted building, neat and quiet on the neat and quiet street. Ernest moved along the stream of sunlight falling up the pavement. A woman was walking two spaniels. Out an area-way came a delivery boy, whistling, and started off with his push-cart. Ernest went in.

The small, white, circular lobby, indirectly lighted, was empty; and he stood a moment, absorbed in his thoughts, feeling the artificially cooled air on his face. "There's a good chance," he told himself, "that she won't want to see me. Well, I'll have to see her anyway—"

A door in the circular wall opened and a small, sharp-featured woman in white, wearing a nurse's cap, came out. Seeing Ernest, she stopped by the small desk at the end, looking at his clerical clothes with stony surprise. When he had told her who he was and what he wanted, she sat down behind the desk, saying, "I'll have to telephone Doctor Stevens before I can let you go upstairs." She asked him for his name again and wrote it on a slip of paper.

"I don't like this place," Ernest thought, able suddenly to guess a good deal about it. He heard the woman saying ". . . a man, a minister, who says he has an appointment . . . very well." She slid a finger under the edge of her desk and pressed a button.

After a while the door in the curved wall, opposite the

one she had come out, opened from the inside, disclosing a long deep elevator. "Six, William. Miss Perkins," the woman said.

The operator was a grave, watchful, no longer young, but stolid and powerful man. He confirmed Ernest in his guess. The simple, expensive fittings, the impregnable silence—mounting, the elevator made not a sound; there was not a sound as they passed the floor doors—were portentous. Ernest knew all about it. There would be only a few patients—men of prominence whose addiction to cocaine must be broken without anyone ever suspecting that they had used it; women of position or celebrity whose attempted suicide must not be dreamed of while they were recovering from what they had done to themselves—the shame, the folly, the fatuity of their desperate evasion hung over them.

When the elevator reached the sixth floor, the operator fastened back the gate and came into the hall with Ernest. He said nothing at all, simply walking ahead until he reached the door he wanted. He knocked on it. When he was told to come in, he opened it.

The room was a large one, furnished as little like a hospital as possible. Although the windows, closed against the outside noise and heat, faced south and were in shadow, they were so wide that the room was full of clear light. On the broad bed Geraldine lay flat on her back, a low pillow hardly raising her head. A magazine was open on the sheet near her extended hand, but she lay still, her eyes closed. It was apparent that she had been expecting, from the knock, a nurse or some attendant. The elevator operator, just behind him, waited a moment while Ernest said, "Geraldine."

Her eyes opened. "Oh," she said, recoiling a little, "Ernie—"

The door was drawn closed, and Ernest went up to the bed. He took the hand lying by the open magazine, patted it. At once she drew it away. She said stiffly: "Thank you for the flowers."

They were on the dressing table. Now that he saw them, he could smell them, mingling with a slight scent of cologne on the cool, quiet air. Without irony, simply thoughtful, he was obliged to remember Mrs. Hawley's room that hot morning. He said, "Are you all right, my dear?"

"I'm all right." She spoke with husky abruptness. "It's all right. I don't like it here much."

"Neither do I," said Ernest. "I know what you don't like. But they'll take good care of you, I think. You'll forget about it."

She had closed her eyes again and he stood gazing at her. Her face was almost wax-colored—he supposed, from the anesthetic used in the morning. Shut, her eyes looked deeply circled, bruised. The dark lids shone as though rubbed with vaseline. She lay perfectly still, but he could see the rapid rise and fall of her breast under the crossed flaps of a silk bed jacket, and while he watched, she parted her lips a little to breathe faster. Then she tightened her eyes, turned her head aside, and immediately he could see the much clearer shine of tears between the lids.

"No, no," he said. "It really is all right."

He walked around the foot of the bed and stood by the windows, looking at the afternoon light laid over the roof tops, at the fine dust and city smoke in a far-off shining horizon haze. Out of it lifted the hot blue, deeper and cleaner as he looked higher. He could hear her begin to sob quietly, with a rough, wincing restraint, as though it hurt her. "I hate him," she said. "I hate him! It's so awful here—"

He turned around and she said, "Oh, God, Ernie, won't you go away?"

"That wouldn't make it any better." He sat down in the armchair and found himself a cigarette. "Geraldine," he said, "there's no reason for me to go away. It isn't likely that you'll ever see me again. Of course I know all about it. But I know it as a priest, my dear. Not as a man, not as an acquaintance you will have to go on facing. So you don't have to feel that way."

She brought a hand up to her breast and pressed it while she made an effort to catch her breath. She said indistinctly, "Yes, I have to. I know someone knows—" Her face twisted and she turned it the other way. She put her knuckles to her mouth. "No, I couldn't ever see you again. I couldn't see anyone. I'm such a damned rotten little fool—"

"You know it," Ernest said. "I know it. God knows it. On me it doesn't make much impression. Lord, the things I've known in my time! I think I've forgotten most of them. I try to. Usually they signify very little about a person. It's more important to know what he does every day. This business isn't like you at all. Very soon we'll both forget it. We're taught that God forgives it."

"What good is that?" she said. "I couldn't forgive myself. I couldn't. I won't ever feel the same again. I can't think of myself the same way—" Her hand searched blindly until it closed on a handkerchief under the corner of the pillow. She lifted it and brushed it across her eyes. She opened them and looked at Ernest. "I can't stand it, Ernie. I could kill him! I could kill myself—"

"That's why I'm sitting here," Ernest said. "Because you can stand it. You're not going to kill anyone, or want to." He smiled. "You can't forgive yourself because you're not entitled to forgive yourself. The good of God is that, if you approach with a pure heart and humble voice, forgiveness will be given you." He looked at the cigarette end between his fingers. "I don't think the way you thought of yourself could have been a way worth keeping. If, from time to time, you find yourself remembering this, it won't hurt you—well, I'll risk the pure heart. I want to hear the humble voice."

"I suppose he couldn't help it," she said. "I suppose it was my fault. Maybe I won't think about it often. I couldn't ever feel that way again. There's that, I suppose. It was like a tearing, Ernie—" She looked at him, surprised, arrested. "You wouldn't ever know," she said. "It's really like having a child—something like it, more like it. You don't believe me, do you?"

"Easily," said Ernest. "I've suffered from ambition, from shame, from despair. You have to describe it in terms of your experience. Unless you keep silent."

She looked at him with an intense, frowning attention and suddenly she said, "Why are you in the Church? Why did you go into it?"

Ernest returned her look a moment. He answered at last. "There are so many reasons. I was temperamentally fitted for it. There was a priest I greatly admired who influenced me. Though not intentionally. I don't think he regarded me as promising. I did many things that were good for me because I hoped to change his mind. There were any number of influences."

"Tell me."

"My father was a severe man—and not at all religious, by the way. I mean, he was unyielding. I think it must have been a great surprise and pleasure to me when I discovered that most people were pliable, that I could work on them. I think I must have felt very sure that I could and would. Not because I could then. I couldn't. I wasn't at all a natural leader. I was just proud and incompetent. I didn't shine at school. I wasn't happy at home. I was too light and small to be good at sports. My father was principal of a high school and had an exaggerated sense of his position and dignity. I daresay I shared it. It was important, because it made him live beyond his means. So I never had any pocket money and, although my mother was a good Churchwoman, that was the real reason I sang in the choir at All Saints'. We were paid twenty cents a week. It led me naturally, when I was old enough, into the Acolytes' Guild. I found I could shine there. In short, the Church gave me an opening. I saw it."

"You mean," she said doubtfully, "that that was all?"

"Isn't it enough?" Ernest asked. He smiled. "It seems to me to be. It's the best way to tell it. It can be understood by people who are satisfied with chance as a sufficient cause. To those who have faith in the miraculous, and believe that there is a purpose in the world, it is just as purposeful and miraculous as the conversion of Saint Paul."

"You mean, it just happened?"

"Can you conceive of that?" he asked. "A year ago could you have dreamed where you would be today? A year ago, was there one chance in a million that I would ever exchange a word with you? Only in God's omniscience. Here you are. Here am I."

She continued to look at him. "You do mean, then," she said, "that really you believe God meant you to be a priest?"

"Just as He means everything to be, that is."

She looked at him, troubled. She hesitated a moment and said, "Even this—I mean, about—"

In the room the shadow was deepening. Over the unlimited acres of roofs the descending sunlight shone a stronger yellow. At the horizon the haze was toned with a faint violet.

Ernest thought: "As sure as night. When it is shown me,

I see. And how little ahead of her I am!" He said, "This is the answer. A great obligation has been laid on me to do or be whatever good thing I have learned I ought to be, or know I can do. I can't excuse myself from it. I dare not bury it or throw it away." He was silent a moment. "One like it is laid on you. You know your obligation, Geraldine. It has always been, to go home and do what your life has prepared you to do. It is all right. Now, you can. Take your talent and employ it—"

He was silent again for a moment, thinking of that terrible twenty-fifth chapter of Saint Matthew's gospel—the untrimmed lamps, the unprofitable servant, the Shepherd enthroned. She looked at him, silent, absorbed, and he began to repeat: "For the kingdom of heaven is as a man traveling into a far country—"

He could hear his voice, calm and clear in the twilight, see her quieted eyes on him "—who called his own servants," he went on, "and delivered unto them his goods. . . ."

D F   Bonett, John
Bon
No Time to Kill